FREUD, JUNG,
& Spiritual Psychology

FREUD, JUNG,
& Spiritual Psychology

RUDOLF STEINER

Five Lectures held in

Dornach and Munich between

February 25, 1912, and July 2, 1921

Translated by May Laird-Brown

Translation revised by Sabine H. Seiler and Richard Smoley

ANTHROPOSOPHIC PRESS

The lectures in this book were published from stenographic records not edited by the lecturer. "Psychoanalysis and Spiritual Psychology I" and "Psychoanalysis and Spiritual Psychology II" appear in German in *Individuelle Geistwesen und ihr Wirken in der Seele des Menschen* (Vol. 178 in the *Collected Works*). "Subconscious and Suptaconscious" and "Hidden Depths of Soul" were published in German in *Erfahrungen des übersinnlichen: Die Wege der Seele zu Christus* (Vol. 143 in the *Collected Works*). "Organic Processes and Soul Life" can be found in German in *Menschenwerden, Weltenseele und Weltengeist* (Vol. 205 in the *Collected Works*). All three titles are published by Rudolf Steiner Verlag in Dornach, Switzerland.

This work was previously published under the titles *Psychoanalysis in the Light of Anthroposophy*, copyright ©1946, and *Psychoanalysis and Spiritual Psychology*, ©1990 Anthroposophic Press.

The quotations from C.G. Jung's work are taken from *Collected Works of C.G. Jung, Vol. 7: Two Essays on Analytical Psychology*. Trans. R.F.C. Hull. Copyright ©1953 Princeton University Press; ©1981 renewed by Princeton University Press. Excerpts from pp.12, 20, 80, 81 reprinted by permission of Princeton University Press.

Published by Anthroposophic Press
P.O. Box 799, Great Barrington, MA 01230
Copyright ©2001 Anthroposophic Press, Inc.
www.anthropress.org

Library of Congress Cataloging-in-Publication Data
Steiner, Rudolf, 1861-1925.
    Freud, Jung, and Spiritual Psychology: five lectures held in Dornach and Munich between February 25, 1912, and July 2, 1921, Rudolf Steiner; translated by May Laird-Brown; translation revised by Sabine H. Seller and Richard Smoley.
    Rev. ed. of: Psychoanalysis in the Light of Anthroposophy. 1946; and Psychoanalysis and Spiritual Psychology, 1990.
    Includes bibliographical references.
    ISBN 0-88010-492-9
        1. Anthroposophy.   2. Psychoanalysis and religion. I. Steiner, Rudolf, 1861-1925. Psychoanalysis in the light of anthroposophy.
        II. Title.

Book Design and Typography: Paul Perlow/Paul Perlow Design

Printed in the United States of America
10 9 8 7 6 5 4 3 2 1

CONTENTS

INTRODUCTION
Robert J. Sardello

WE LIVE IN an age when psychotherapy in its myriad forms is taken for granted. Imagine, just for a moment, how many people in the world practice psychotherapy, how many are patients of one therapy or another, and how many are now involved in the growing numbers of therapeutic groups focused on various addictions. One might think that a great deal of "soul work" goes on here. But, due to fundamental errors at the very founding of the discipline, it may well be that psychotherapy is oriented toward conquering soul rather than entering into soul wisdom. By "soul wisdom" I mean the capacity of self-knowledge based on the development of the practice of a fully conscious meditative awareness leading to a picture-consciousness that "sees through" experience of both inner and outer worlds to the activity of spiritual beings. These lectures on psychoanalysis and spiritual psychology, given by Rudolf Steiner in the years 1912, 1917, and 1921, at the very time when the "talking cure" was in its beginnings, force us to confront the inadequate knowledge used in founding psychoanalysis and psychotherapy as a method of soul work. Now, some eighty years later, this method has multiplied endlessly, and without questioning the kind of knowing involved. Arguments can be found pitting one school of therapy against another, but I can think of only one contemporary analyst, James Hillman, who questions the whole enterprise. Hillman bases his critique on the astute observation that, by sequestering it in a private room, therapy removes soul from the world and thereby degrades its intricacies. The result, he says, is a world lacking the sense of soul. Now, exactly how psychotherapy got into this situation and how it contributes to a culture lacking in soul can be learned by following Steiner's exploration of the development of psychoanalysis.

Step one: The nature of a wound of the soul, of inner life, was misread very early on in the history of psychoanalysis. Consequently, instead of learning how to pay attention to soul, psychoanalysis was diverted to the supposed circumstances in which the wounding occurred — circumstances that were said to take place during the historical life of the person. Thereby, with a brilliant move of ordinary intelligence, Freud sidestepped the opportunity to develop a kind of knowledge suitable for the soul. That is to say, he did not see that the appearance of psychological symptoms, a new phenomenon of the age, points to the need for the development of new capacities of perception. Psychological symptoms indicate that the boundary between consciousness and subconsciousness has become unreliable, that the lower soul forces have begun to penetrate into ordinary consciousness, producing disruption because there are no forms for this new experience. New capacities of perception would mean the development of moral, aesthetic, and intellectual qualities — qualities that would broaden and deepen the middle realm of the soul, and could then enter into culture for further development. Instead, Freud contended that a person's suffering is not due to the wounding but to the inability to understand what is happening within what Steiner would call sense-perceptible knowledge. Psychoanalysis helps the suffering patient to achieve this form of understanding by associating the wounds of the soul with historical events in the person's life; once the wounding "makes sense," relief occurs.

Psychoanalysis in this sense is a training in making the soul conform to the scientific analysis of cause and effect, an education into materialist logic which undoubtedly goes hand in hand with learning to view the events of the outer world with this same kind of logic.

Step two: Once a theory of causation is established the psychoanalytic researcher, in good scientific fashion, must look for a principle that accounts for all cases of the phenomenon. Freud found this in the principle of sexuality — that behind all neuroses lies a wounding brought about by a trauma of love. This step is one further departure from the soul because it is an abstraction separated from the life of the person as a whole. Interestingly, the current popularity of addiction and codependency groups even more strongly reinforces this departure from the nature of the soul which culminates with Alice Miller's work, *The Drama of the Gifted Child*. Here Freud's starting point, which is the present experience of a wound of the soul, is completely disregarded, and the original wound is now taken to be an actual wound in the historical life of the person. The difference is crucial. While Freud avoided investigating soul directly through developing a means of perception that would give such knowledge, he nevertheless never took the stories told by patients to be actual accounts of the past; he took them to be memories, and, as such, filled with fictional elaboration. In the new version, soul is taken out of the picture altogether, and now literally thousands and thousands of persons come together weekly in groups to discuss the historical events of their wounding at the hands of abusive parents. From there they are led into the Twelve-Step recovery program, into a dependency on one's self-selected version of a "higher power," as if one could get to the spirit by completely bypassing soul. The vessel is now completely broken. The eruption of soul experiences, a cultural phenomenon of the age, is again suppressed, and the possibility of developing a true knowledge of the inner life is thereby decreased.

Now what is the inner life? Talking about one's feelings, recovering early childhood memories, delving into emotions, describing personal experiences — none of this concerns the inner life. There is a story told concerning the writer Balzac that when he was on his deathbed, many of his associates and friends came to see him, as if to get a last word from the master. Balzac would ask these people about certain other people — how they were doing in life, how their marriages were faring, whether a certain person ever got out of his trouble with the law. Balzac, however, was not talking about actual people. He was talking about the characters in his novels. This is the true inner life, when the goings-on of the inner world become as real as any outer event. True wisdom of the soul would seek to develop this kind of strength of inner perception, not to cure it.

Psychoanalysis and all its offshoots have a further, more far-reaching effect than simple ineffectiveness in encouraging a genuine inner life. Once a theory of the unconscious is established, an iatrogenic disease of the psyche ensues. That is, the cure of the illness becomes the source of illness. The theories themselves, Steiner points out, agitate the subconscious, and in this manner, what begins as a limited field of inquiry spreads into a cultural phenomenon. That is to say, psychotherapy is a self-perpetuating phenomenon; the more it is done the more illness is created.

The student of psychological systems might think that the

difficulties pointed out thus far may be true for Freud and
those psychotherapeutic approaches that can be linked back
to him, but that with Jung there occurs a real breakthrough
into the realm of the soul proper. Not only does Jung break
with Freud's sexual foundation, but he sees the limitation of
personal memory, realizing that symptoms cannot be
accounted for by simply following the events of early childhood, and that there exists a whole other realm of memory,
the collective unconscious, which seems to be the image presentation of the soul world. Mythic memory, not personal
memory, becomes with Jung the source of psychological illness. The gods, Jung says, have become our diseases. The difficulty, according to him, is that the mythic content stirring
within the soul, when it is not conscious, causes illness.
Relief comes when conscious connection is made with these
mythic stirrings. The gods are necessary to human beings, but
simply as a psychological function. The psychology of Jung,
therefore, does not open perception to spiritual reality; it
stops short. The cultural result here is more complex than in
the case of Freud. The legacy of Jung has led to a psychology
of abstractions — anima, animus, projection, shadow, intro-
version, extraversion — which do their share of creating illness, but in a different way than with Freud. Rather than
focusing on the historicity of the soul wound, the legacy of
Jung produces instead a wholly subjective psychology in
which the gods are reduced to the familiarity of ordinary cognition, set into dramatic interplay by abstract concepts acting
as if they were real. Furthermore, patients in this kind of psychoanalysis become students of those amateur mythologists,
the analysts themselves, who set about convincing their
patients that they are walking texts upon whom are written

the stories of the gods which they do not know they are enacting in their lives. Once they become willing carriers of these
gods and goddesses, symptoms are relieved. An important
exception to this tendency is to be found in the work of James
Hillman, whose work is indebted to Jung, but who refuses to
engage in such tomfoolery. The archetypal psychology of
Hillman takes the imaginal world to be fully objective and
real. But, as I have already indicated, this leads him to reject
the notion of therapy.

I see the influence of Jung working in two directions in our
culture. On the one hand, it has fostered an imitation religion,
the conception of Jung as a mystic, and the elevation of subjectivity to the status of religious experience. That is to say,
inadequate cognition becomes honored as religion. It produces
bad art and a form of ritual in which individuals worship
themselves thinking they are honoring some deity, and dreams
are treated as sacred texts. On the other hand, Jung's cultural
influence has brought about a peculiar interest in myth, exem-
plified most clearly by Joseph Campbell, in which myth is
reduced to the terms of ordinary consciousness. Campbell, I
propose, is not a mythologist but a demythologizer, faithfully
explaining to millions of television viewers the workings of
myth in terms that require nothing of the viewer, coupled with
the sentimentality of the wonders of lost worlds. Interpreting
myth, as Campbell does, differs considerably from mythologi-
cal thinking. The former stands outside the myth while the
latter appreciates and practices it by moral investigation; that
is, it recognizes that myth demands a response in the present.
It approaches myth as the symbolic expression of correspon-
dences between prototypes above and their manifestations
below. Campbell, conversely, approaches myth as the symbol-

ic expression of archetypes in the past, with the result that one only learns what has been lost and is not directed toward seeing these expressions in new forms occurring in present circumstances. Jung mixed and confused prototype and archetype without knowing he was doing so.

In the middle of the second of this series of lectures, Steiner makes a statement that is not a mere observation but a report of something he saw by way of supersensible faculties concerning the life of Nietzsche. It is quite astounding, Steiner says — and we also know this from other places in his writings — that Wagner, after his death, was the spiritual guide of Nietzsche. Then, however, Steiner says that Wagner allowed Nietzsche to become mentally deranged to protect him from entering consciously into dangerous regions of spirit. What might have occurred, we must consider, had Nietzsche had the benefit of psychotherapy? What forces would have been loosed on the world? Does not psychotherapy sanction a truly terrible hubris when it treats the situation of the soul as if it were diseased? Is it not hubris when the analyst determines that what the patient is given to confront in life is the wrong thing for that person to confront, or is being confronted in the wrong way? One cannot, however, even consider such a possibility without the benefit of true spiritual perception. In truth, the psychotherapist has not the faintest notion of what he is dealing with or of how very simplistic even the most complex of psychological theories really are because of the failure to recognize the reality of the spiritual worlds. For instance, even when a transpersonal dimension seems to be taken into account, as with Jung, the individual soul is never considered beyond the life between birth and death. Spiritual cognition, on the other hand, sees feelings as carried over from the soul life of the period of an individual's last death to this birth, while will is seen as the soul life of the previous incarnation. Current psychology is capable of seeing these qualities of soul only as limited to individual life between birth and death.

The real dangers of psychotherapy are exposed when the full spiritual nature of the human being is brought to light. The key to the full cognition of individual human reality lies in reincarnation, which for Steiner is not an idea but a matter of spiritual perception. I hope that the reader who is encountering anthroposophy for the first time will be led to study Steiner's researches concerning reincarnation. With respect to the question of psychotherapy, it is most important to gain an understanding concerning what I would call the porosity of the soul between death and rebirth. By porosity, I mean that the soul life during the period between death and birth and the soul life of previous incarnations permeate and are permeated with the whole spirit world. Soul is not isolated within itself: it extends into the whole spirit world. In the life between birth and death this means that feeling and will are not isolated within the individual soul, are not a purely individual matter. Symptoms, then — and this is what is so hard for us to accept because of the all-pervasive acceptance of psychology as concerning the subjectivity of soul — do not belong to the individual but to the culture as a whole; they are individually lived aspects of the milieu in which one lives. Furthermore, symptoms indicate the needed direction for knowledge of the spiritual world that must be taken by the culture as a whole. Symptoms do not simply call for the effort to ameliorate individual suffering, as if the world in which such suffering occurs does not matter. Let me provide an example, that of addictions.

Within our addictions lies the expectation of magical, ritual, and spiritual transformation. One gives oneself over to a
substance that comes from afar and is supposed to carry one
far away. The exotic drug is a metaphor for wisdom and psy-
chic/spiritual experience, a metaphor indicating a longing for
spirit. The process of addiction involves three components,
only two of which are presently recognized. First, a physical,
organic habit is formed. Then a more subtle habit develops
which forms itself into a kind of conditioning. The silent,
unrecognized component is a striving, an unfruitful quest for
spiritual experience. Drug addictions, moreover, point to a
much larger field of addictions to virtually anything — substances, other people, position, knowledge, pleasure, money,
power, possessions, sex, recognition. Addictions indicate a
taking-in of the materialistic world view, as if possessing the
world would produce completeness of spirit. As a spiritual
symptom of the age, however, addictions indicate that today's
spiritual task is to develop the capacities to experience the
world in a more spiritual way, to actually find spirit in the
world through a relation to the world that develops the perception of spiritual activities occurring there. Working with
addiction as an individual problem or enacting laws and leg-
islation misses seeing the spiritual task of the time. The task
does not direct us to some abstract idea of spirit or equally
abstract idea of learning to ask for guidance from a higher
power, but directs us to develop a spiritual cognition of the
world that does not depart from the particularity of every
individual thing of the world.

Anthroposophy leads to a wisdom of the soul and is thus
never content to stop with the act of careful examination of
limited systems of knowledge. While Steiner agrees that the

phenomena originating psychoanalysis are of critical importance, he says that because Freud did not recognize spirit, soul became identified with individual history, which led to a view of history without soul. This development of the psychoanalytic model indicates that the soul is not sufficient unto itself. It is part of spirit and therefore can be investigated by the means of spiritual research. Now I want to show how such investigation differs from psychoanalysis. This difference is actually more subtle than one might think, for there seem to be close similarities. In order to perceive the difference, therefore, it is necessary to avoid all abstraction.

First, the spiritual investigator must learn that there is a difference between one's own inner life and the experience of the objective spiritual world. Avoiding this crucial difference leads on the one hand to the confused mysticism of Jung, and on the other to modern psychologists such as R.D. Laing, who approach schizophrenia as if it were spiritual experience. The first reduces spiritual experience to subjective psychology; the second enlarges subjective experience beyond its proper domain. Only the spiritual cognition of the life of the soul can produce the kind of knowledge that avoids such confusions — a knowledge of the difference between soul that is self-enclosed and soul that is permeated with and radiates into the objective spiritual world, the difference between subconsciousness and supraconsciousness. One might think that Jung made this distinction, that he recognized the supraconscious realm with his more mystical investigations of the archetype of the Self. But the Self may be no more than mystical megalomania, whereby one sees the divine only within oneself or identifies the ordinary, empirical self with the higher Self and then the higher Self with God. True, Jung fully recognized this danger and called it inflation. He gave warnings, but no way of distinguishing. Further, the explorations of the archetype of the Self, and along with it the process of so-called individuation, never lead to the multiplicity and particularity of the spiritual worlds, but only to abstractions such as oneness and wholeness — terms we are now endlessly subjected to in popular spirituality.

The work of distinguishing sub- and supraconsciousness must occur before — not after — their fusion, and the distinction is not one of ideas, but of a feeling for what is real. Steiner tells us how to go about this task. This is something that must be actually done, not just read about. You will find in the text, for example, the procedure of picturing a double of yourself arranging all the circumstances that brought about in your life what you did not wish to happen but which happened nonetheless. The result of this crucial experiment — this careful attention to experience — gives a very solid feeling of how soul brings about what needs to happen to us. By experiencing all we do not desire as what we do desire, we prepare ground for releasing the soul from its imprisonment in itself. Now we find this theme to be also quite popular in new age spirituality; in a certain sense it is also present in the Twelve-Step programs of the addiction and codependency movements, where it is called being "responsible." But surely such language fosters further imprisonment in the self. In addition, the addiction program says that nothing within me was responsible for what happened to me as a child in the past. Once I clear away the rage at what was done to me by others, only from this point on can I take responsibility for what happens to me. All egotism and no soul. And yet we see within this modern procedure a longing for something for which we have no tools, no language. One must develop a real feeling for the enclosure of the soul within itself during the period after death when the soul's life-experience is displayed before itself as if it were an objective world. And one must develop a real feeling for the soul's full engagement in the spiritual worlds — which are not of the soul's making — that occurs after this first period following death. One does not have to be clairvoyant to do so; we have intimations of these experiences even in daily life. Then karma becomes no longer a spiritual buzzword but an actual experience of the soul's suffering and of how this suffering can be endured in time as the universal solvent and taken up as a spiritual task — a task that is not for personal benefit but has the aim of collaborating with the forces of the spiritual worlds.

Anthroposophy not only takes us out of the limited domain of psychology as concerned with subjective states and into the broader realm of culture, it also takes us into an understanding of the body as the necessary organ through which spiritual perception must find its orientation. Psychology still suffers from the legacy of its official namer, Philipp Melanchthon, who narrowed psyche to subjectivity. From the point of view of this legacy, it matters not whether that subjectivity is conscious or unconscious; the body is not considered except insofar as it is affected by the psyche, as if psyche were not of the body. Steiner's comprehension of the historical development of consciousness, however, places what is now called psyche in the realm of the sentient soul and thus it belongs to the body and the organs of the body. Great confusion arises due to the fact that matters of the sentient soul are treated as if they were matters of the intellectual soul. Compare, for example, Heraclitus, who said, "You could not discover the limits of the psyche, even if you traveled every road to do so," with Melanchthon: "We divide man into only two parts. For there is in him a cognitive faculty, and there is also a faculty by which he either follows or flees the things he has come to know. The cognitive faculty is that by which we discern through the senses, understand, think, compare, and deduce. The faculty from which the affections arise is that by which we either turn away from or pursue the things known, and this faculty is sometimes called 'will,' sometimes 'affection,' and sometimes 'appetite.'" Now take Melanchthon and start talking about the gods and goddesses, and you have the kind of intellectual gossip about the gods characteristic of much current popular psychology that speaks about the gods and goddesses within — a very peculiar, confused mixture of fabulous tales and pop subjectivity with spiritual overtones. When this kind of fare becomes commonplace, spiritual wisdom sounds incomprehensible, whereas in fact the reverse is true: nonsense has taken the place of accurate perception. Thus a first encounter with the latter essays of this collection may be met with difficulty at first because it is necessary to counter a great deal of cultural conditioning. The key lies in realizing that Steiner speaks meditatively; consequently one is required to work with what is presented by first reading the essays as a whole, suspending what one thinks one already knows, and then thinking through the particularities of the whole in an attitude of meditation.

When the body is not divided from the psyche, an account must be given first of everyday consciousness, and then of those perceptions that are not available to everyday consciousness, not only dreams, but also all those phenomena that form the field of so-called abnormal psychology. What makes consciousness possible is not the brain as a producer of consciousness, but the processes of the body as a whole. These serve as a mirror reflecting the activity of the soul. You can never arrive at the spiritual dimension by starting with material processes; a dualism will always result. But it is possible, when the starting place is soul and spirit, to show the necessity of the body in relation to soul and spirit; it is not a matter of concocting an idea, but of paying attention to what is actually given to experience. Goethe's theory of colors, for example, is such an instance of careful attention to experience that shows the activity of the soul. When one stares at a blue spot for a few moments and then closes one's eyes, a yellow afterimage of the spot is seen. Physiology cannot adequately account for the phenomenon that whenever an outer color is seen, an afterimage of the complementary color is seen simultaneously. (When one looks at the blue spot for a time, a pulsating yellow emanates around the spot.) The soul activity of the blood (see Ernst Lehrs, *Man or Matter*) creates the complementary, and thus makes color perception possible. This exemplary instance gives a feeling for what happens in all of ordinary everyday consciousness. That is to say, consciousness is a phenomenon of soul requiring body. It is not a result of a stimulation of the bodily nerves being transmitted to the brain which then produces the experience.

But in addition to being the reflector for everyday consciousness, the body is also the reflector for all that arises from the depths of the soul unrelated to outer experience. Spiritual training is oriented toward entering these depths with proper discrimination. With Steiner's approach to these matters we have the foundation for an entirely new direction for abnormal psychology, one based on the reality of spiritual worlds and the soul's progress from one incarnation to another. Abnormal psychology, then, becomes a primary mode for researching the processes of reincarnation. Furthermore, care of soul changes radically when one's vision is expanded to include not only past lives but also, more importantly, future lives. Indeed, Steiner's perception of the relation of the bodily organs as expressions of the soul to psychological irregularities is particularly oriented toward care of the soul, with a view toward future lives. He sees that psychological difficulties arise when something that is to be lived in a future incarnation is, so to speak, squeezed out of a bodily organ in this life, producing disruption. To state the matter in this way sounds fantastic, but that is so only if such a proposition is heard without knowledge of the higher worlds. Thus an adequate training in spiritual science is required to follow this line of research, and the aim of sketching out the approach of anthroposophy is to stimulate the impulse to take up this direction of work.

Steiner considers in these essays the following organs in relation to psychological irregularities. Remember, however, that he is not proposing a cause-effect relationship, as if when there is physical organ damage this causes a particular form of abnormality — he is not putting forth a psychosomatic theory, for all such theories are dualistic. Rather it is the case that the bodily organs as living body processes act as reflectors of psychic activity. The lung surface serves as reflector of abstract concepts, and also of thoughts concerned with perception of the outer world. The lungs, and this is immediately available to experience, have to do with the ongoing exchange between the outer world and inner life. When the forces of the lungs are too strongly stimulated, the result is coercive thoughts or illusions; what should be the head-forming forces of the next incarnation are expressed as overpowering thought. The liver surface reflects thoughts colored by feelings; indeed, the liver is the organ which, even in its name, means "life." What should form the inner forces of the brain in the next life, if pressed out in this life, are lived as hallucinations and visions. The forces of the kidneys, concerned with excretion, when forced to pour these out in this life, instead of preparing the emotional organization of the following life, express themselves as hypochondria and depression. The heart as a spiritual organ concerns the spiritualization of life processes and conscience, our deeds. Our deeds carry our karma into the next life, and if the forces of the heart are activated in the wrong manner a kind of frenzy results. What Steiner speaks of as frenzy, I suspect, is what modern psychology would call obsession. Obsession is a malady of our age, a cultural phenomenon characterized by the idealized thought of relationship enacted as deed without the restraint that would produce hesitation of action.

The nuances of Steiner's development of these forms of illness are well worth study and contemplation. This way of approaching psychological phenomena completely shifts the perception of psychology, and indeed are the foundation for a true spiritual psychology. Now within this context, what of psychotherapy — does it have a place at all? Probably not, for this way of seeing soul work does not in any way diminish the difficulty previously pointed to — that what should occur in life, psychotherapy places in the interaction between two or more individuals in an artificial situation, which is an incursion into the karma of an individual. Care for the soul, however, is something that can be practiced by the individual. The fundamental reason psychotherapy is such a dubious practice is that karma is moral, and thus feeling and willing are moral activities of the soul. They are the way soul works on itself, producing exactly what is to be experienced in exactly the right way and time in life. If one proceeds abstractly, then it could be said, Well, when one gets to real stumbling blocks in life and is in a really impossible situation that leads to the door of the psychotherapist, that too is to be considered karma. Such a point of view, however, is a naíve abstraction because it takes a cultural invention, psychotherapy, and treats this idea as if it were something belonging to life; but it does not belong to life; rather, it is an artificially arranged situation that places people together in a form that imitates the most intimate aspects of life.

What then could be put forward as a true alternative? After all, psychological suffering is undeniable, and to ignore it would be like saying that when thousands of people undergo the devastation of an earthquake, that is their karma. It would be ludicrous not to help these people, even though it is quite true that those who find themselves in the exact time and place of an earthquake are confronting karma. First, it is necessary to locate psychological suffering as a cultural phenomenon and to bring about knowledge of the spirit suitable to present cultural circumstances. Such knowledge of the spirit must not be abstract, but capable of addressing the actual situation of our times. Anthroposophy forms such a method of knowledge; however, it is not yet psychology, though it implicitly carries a psychological dimension. Knowledge of the spirit becomes psychological knowledge when the focus is on the body — not only the individual human body, but equally the body of things and the body of the world, what in the ancient world was called the *anima mundi*, or "soul of the world." The focus, of course, is not only on the physical body — training in spiritual science awakens the sense of the living body (physical, etheric, astral, ego) and of the relation between the living macrocosm and the living microcosm. The critical point, however, is this: the endeavor to bring about a true spiritual psychology belongs to the realm of education rather than psychotherapy. Why is this so? There is nothing whatsoever within the human being that would call forth from the processes of life such a particular cultivation of life as what is called psychotherapy.

Friendship and the intimacy of a love relationship may come to mind, but neither of these forms of being human takes place in an isolated chamber, and even friends and lovers do not know what a therapist knows because he knows what he should not. Self-knowledge is an unbreachable intimacy one has with one's soul. Certain cultural expressions, which I shall speak of in a moment, can awaken an awareness of the necessity of self-knowledge and the path toward this knowledge, but even these expressions cannot substitute for the complete individuality of self-knowledge. Psychotherapy is an abstraction, culturally sanctioned in a world of materialistic abstractions. Learning, however, does belong to the very nature of living. Let me give an indication concerning how learning belongs to living; then it will be possible to propose the particular kind of education required for spiritual psychology.

The impulse for learning originates in an alluring display of the beauty of the world, evoking desire for intimate connection with the world — an urge toward the spirit, soul, vitality, the particular beauty marking each thing as standing forth from a holy abyss. Things draw us to intimate knowledge as if they need us for their completion. The beauty of the world draws the soul out of a self-enclosing illusion of mastery through disengagement into an engagement with reality. This living desire to experience the world pulsing through the body constitutes a drive toward transformation, initiating a care for all things. When things are approached with the care of the soul, their spiritual reality shines forth. The central task of learning is not the accumulation of information, but is learning to learn, that is, coming to realize the individual body in conjunction with the body of the world as the container and reflector of soul processes. Now this process of learning cannot be divided into those who learn and those who teach. Teachers are simply those whose vocation is learning, those who have learned that life is learning. When educators recognize this force, the spiritual/cultural necessity of learning will take its rightful precedence over technical and social concerns.

The phenomena of abnormal psychology, when seen within this context of learning as essential to life, lead not to psychotherapy but to adult education: spiritual psychology as the field of adult learning. That is to say, the missing element in contemporary culture is an education into the life of spirit. This form of learning does not really belong to the young. Education in the seven liberal arts is the field of learning for the young; in ancient times, the study of the liberal arts — grammar, dialectic, rhetoric, geometry, arithmetic, astronomy, and music — was the preparation needed for spiritual knowledge. I propose that what Freud and Jung observed as the manifestation of psychological symptoms was simply the disappearance from the world of a culture of soul and spirit. Cultural forms are needed for the cure; psychotherapy cannot do the job and seems to me a deviation contributing to the destruction of culture.

Spiritual psychology as the field of adult education certainly does not mean adult education in the current sense of the practice; presently, adult education is oriented either toward furtherance of technical skills or toward personal enrichment. Where then is an education of the soul to be found today? There isn't one, because the imitation, the double, of such a task occurs as psychotherapy. That is to say, self-knowledge has no culture. Adult education, then, would restore to culture knowledge of the soul. Its method would be quite different from education of the young, for the task of cultural learning in this sense lies much more in the hands of the learners and with the community of learners. The teacher is not as important in a certain sense. He or she must be skilled enough to recede into the background while nonetheless serving as a guide who can help shape the vessel and restrain the learning from wandering into personal subjectivity. Adult education is community learning, but is in no sense a group psychotherapy. And it is learning to care for soul, explicitly. The method of such learning is meditative rather than intellectual, for soul learning is an education into subtlety. In reading these lectures by Steiner I think it is imperative to have this form of education in mind; otherwise, when he touches upon certain exercises that are needed to come to living knowledge of the soul, it is easy to think, "Well, that can be imported into the work of psychotherapy?" and what Steiner is really pointing toward is a different approach to psychotherapy. Not at all, for then all that he works to bring to light in the early lectures in this series is for naught. Nor, however, do I think Steiner is suggesting that in place of psychotherapy one find a spiritual master who will be one's individual spiritual guide.

Adult education into soul wisdom must also be distinguished from reading or study groups. Such groups tend to be
oriented toward detailed understanding of a particular work
or text and foster a strengthening of the intellectual soul
rather than the consciousness soul. What the teacher of soul
wisdom must first gain and then sacrifice is the development
of the intellectual soul; this is necessary in order that a spirit
of meditative consciousness pervade this new situation of
learning. The way such teaching occurs in practice is that the
teacher actually has much knowledge and information, but
cannot give it forth. He does not withhold it, but brings it into
the learning situation to be given up, in order to, as it were,
provide the context for the meditative learning pursued by the
community of learners. Reading is approached in a similarly
meditative manner. Meditative reading is encouraged that
takes place through picture-consciousness rather than through
the grasping of concepts. That is, the aim of reading and study
is not oriented toward what one can take away from the text
but toward going into it in a living way. Needless to say, this
form of learning is noncompetitive. No evaluation takes place
and no examinations are given, and no grading. These devices
stimulate the wrong forces for soul wisdom.

Is there a curriculum for the soul? A crucial question. Yes,
there is material. but there is not a sequentially arranged form of
studies that progresses from the simple to the more complex.
Secondary texts are avoided, and as well the use of excerpts from
works because the aim is to become immersed not in what is said
about some topic but in the reality itself. The curriculum then is
formed not out of the personal interests of the teacher, but out of
a considered intuition of the teacher in relation to the community of learners concerning the soul development of all involved.

Art is of particular importance for an education into spiritual psychology — myth, fairy tale, story, symbolic image, mandala, poetry, drama, painting, music, and film. Furthermore, art forms that are explicitly made as revelations and expression of spirit, carrying the intention of awakening and initiating the conscious life of spirit, are important. Because the focus is on works of imagination, the middle realm of soul is engaged which thereby affects both body and spirit. Since the works are of a spiritual nature, the lower regions of the soul are educated and what otherwise would be disruptive chaos is given cultural form. Examples of such works include: J.W. von Goethe, *Fairy Tale of the Green Snake and the Beautiful Lily; The Chymical Wedding of Christian Rosenkreutz;* Wolfram von Eschenbach, *Parzival;* Verdi's operas; the major arcana of the tarot; alchemical engravings; Rudolf Steiner, *The Four Mystery Plays;* the paintings of Hieronymus Bosch; the poetry of Novalis; the films of Andrei Tarkovsky; Greek mythology.

Psychological irregularities, in spite of a cultural form of education into soul are, of course, still bound to exist. These instances are to be cared for within the field of medicine: not medicine or psychiatry as currently practiced, not drugs and incarceration and therapy, but medicine with soul. This does not violate culture because medicine is a communal expression of culture. Once the knowledge that intense psychological difficulties are expressions of the forces of the bodily organs is brought forth, then the need for a medicine capable of working with body as soul is apparent. Psychoanalysis originated in a confusion of soul work with medicine, and all current forms of psychotherapy are knowingly or unknowingly pervaded with a medical attitude. One might be led to think that what needs to be brought about is a clearing away of all medical suppositions in psychotherapy, the main one being a diagnostic attitude that begins therapy with the question "What is wrong with you?" Then, it would be possible to have a new form of therapy. When this diagnostic attitude is relinquished, however, what presents itself as psychological disruption is the invasion of unfamiliar images, feelings, thoughts, and actions. Such phenomena make even more apparent the need for cultural forms that can shape disruptive forces into coherent images. In spite of the popular appeal of the romantic attitude that everyone is or can be an artist, only those who have devoted their lives to such tasks are really capable, and, fortunately, they have made cultural artifacts through which we can be led where we cannot go on our own.

The careful reader of these lectures is led into vital considerations of the forming of a more spiritual culture. The conclusions are not easy to confront. They have led me, a practicing psychotherapist, to the necessity of relinquishing this practice. But following through Steiner's wisdom has also led to the founding of an initiative, which I have called adult education into soul wisdom, and that produces a great sense of relief, as well as hope that possibilities will also be released in the reader.

The Dallas Institute of Humanities and Culture
May, 1990

LECTURE ONE
PSYCHOANALYSIS AND SPIRITUAL PSYCHOLOGY I
November 10, 1917

T HROUGH THE LECTURES I am giving now in Zurich, I am freshly reminded that one can hardly encounter the spiritual life of that city without giving some attention to what is now called "analytical psychology" or "psychoanalysis."[1] Various reflections connected with this realization prompt me to introduce what I have to say today with a short discussion of certain points in analytical psychology or psychoanalysis that we will then link with my further remarks.

We have often noted how important it is for researchers in the field of spiritual psychology to connect their studies with what our own age offers. It may be said that all sorts of people who feel drawn to psychoanalysis are earnestly searching for the spiritual foundations of existence, for the inner realities of the human soul. And it is a curious characteristic of our time that so many of our contemporaries are becoming aware of certain peculiar forces in the human soul. The psychoanalysts belong to those who, simply through the impulses of the age, are forced to look at certain phenomena of soul.

It is especially important not to remain entirely oblivious of this movement, because the phenomena it takes into consideration are really present, and in our time they intrude themselves for various reasons upon our attention. Today we *must* become aware of such phenomena.

On the other hand, the people who concern themselves with these things lack the means of knowledge required to discuss and, above all, to understand them. Thus, we may say that psychoanalysis is a phenomenon of our time that compels people to take note of certain soul processes, and yet it leads them to study these processes with inadequate means. It is particularly significant that here the investigation of something that obviously exists and challenges our understanding is based on inadequate methods of knowledge, and that always leads to various serious errors. It can be hazardous to social life and to the further development of knowledge, as well as to the latter's influence on social life.

It may be said that half-truths are, under certain circumstances, more harmful than complete errors. And what the psychoanalysts bring to light today can be regarded only as an assortment of quarter-truths.

Let us consider a few excerpts from the research journal of the psychoanalysts. What is called psychoanalysis today began with a medical case studied by a Vienna intern, a Dr. Breuer, in the 1880s.[2] Dr. Breuer, a physician with whom I was acquainted, had an extraordinarily subtle mind. He was greatly interested in all sorts of aesthetic and general human problems. As he was very thorough and careful in dealing with his patients, it was natural that one of his cases in particular was especially interesting to him.

He had to treat a woman who seemed to be suffering from severe symptoms of hysteria. Her symptoms were a paralysis of one arm, occasional fits of absentmindedness or twilight states, deep drowsiness, and in addition, she had forgotten her native language. She had always been able to speak German; it was her mother tongue, but under the influence of her hysteria she could no longer do so; she could speak and understand only English.

Breuer noticed that during her twilight states, he could persuade her through careful medical treatment to speak of a certain scene, a very trying past experience. Now I will show you, from the description of the case given by the Breuer school, how the woman in her absentminded condition, which was sometimes artificially induced — Breuer could easily hypnotize a patient — was induced to speak of these experiences. What she said gave the impression that her hysteria was connected with her father's illness, through which she had nursed him a long time ago. Her father had been very ill, and she had been helping with the nursing when she had the experience. She spoke again and again of this particular experience, which is described as follows:[3]

> One night, watching by the sick man, who had a high fever, she was tense with anxiety because a surgeon was expected from Vienna to perform an operation. Her mother had left the room for a while, and Anna (the patient) sat by the sickbed with her right arm hanging over the back of the chair. She fell into a sort of waking dream in which she saw a black snake coming, apparently out of the wall, towards the sick man as though to bite him.

Nowadays people usually get a blow on the back of the neck by materialism, and so we find in this report the following comment, by which we do not need to set great store:

> It is quite likely that there really were snakes in the meadow at the back of the house, which had already given the girl a fright and which now provided the material for the hallucination.[4]

That is only an incidental remark. You may attach importance to it, or not; it does not matter. As the patient saw it, the snake came out of the wall to bite her father.

> She wanted to drive the creature away, but felt paralyzed; her right arm, hanging over the back of the chair, had "gone to sleep": it had become anesthetic and paretic, and, as she looked at it, the fingers changed into little serpents with death's heads. Probably she made efforts to drive away the snake with her paralyzed right hand, so that the anesthesia and paralysis became associated with the snake hallucination. When the snake had disappeared, she was so frightened that she wanted to pray; but all speech failed her, she could not utter a word until finally she remembered an English nursery rhyme, and then she was able to go on thinking and praying in English.[5]

The whole illness originated from this experience. From it there had remained the paralysis of one hand, twilight states of various kinds, and the inability to express herself in any language but English. Breuer then noticed that the condition was alleviated whenever he had her tell her story, and he based his treatment upon this fact. Through hypnosis he drew from her little by little all the details and really succeeded in bringing about a marked improvement in her condition. The patient got rid of the problem, as it were, by expressing and communicating it to another person.

Breuer and his collaborator Freud in Vienna were both influenced, as was natural at that time, by the school of Charcot in Paris, and diagnosed this case as a psychic trauma, a psychic wound — what is called in England a "nervous shock."[6] The psychic shock was supposed to have been this experience at her father's bedside, and to have had an effect upon the soul similar to that of a physical wound upon the body.

It must be noted that from the beginning Breuer saw the whole affair as a soul illness, as a matter of the inner life. He was convinced from the beginning that no anatomical or physiological changes could have been shown — for example, no changes in the nerves leading from the arm to the brain. He was convinced from the start that he was dealing with a psychic symptom.

In those early days, researchers were inclined to regard these cases as induced by wounds of the soul, shocks, and the like. Very soon, however, because of Dr. Freud's active interest, theories took on a different character. Breuer was never fully in accord with Freud's further development of the subject. Freud felt that the theory of soul wounds did not fully explain these cases. Breuer also was convinced that simply attributing these illnesses to a wound of the soul was not enough. I would like to point out parenthetically, as it were, that Dr. Breuer was a very busy practicing physician, thoroughly trained in science, an excellent student of Nothnagel, and it was only because of external circumstances that he never became a professor.[7] We may well believe that if Breuer, instead of remaining one of the busiest physicians in Vienna with little time for scientific research, had obtained a professorship and had thus been able to follow up this problem, it might have taken on a very different form!

But from then on Dr. Freud took a special interest in the matter. He realized that the theory of trauma does not explain these cases. It needs to be determined under what conditions such a soul wound affects the patient. After all, it might be said with justice that many people had sat at sickbeds and certainly had equally deep impressions, but without leading to the same results. The unschooled layperson settles such problems promptly with the extraordinarily profound explanation that one person is predisposed to such symptoms while another is not. Although very "profound," this is the most absurd solution one can arrive at, is it not? For if you explain things on the basis of predisposition, you can easily explain everything in the world. All you need to say is that the predisposition for a certain thing exists.

Of course serious thinkers did not concern themselves with such ideas, but sought the real conditions. And Freud believed he had discovered them in cases such as the following. You will find innumerable similar cases in the literature of the psychoanalysts today, and it may be admitted that an immense amount of material has been collected in order to decide this or that point in this field. I will describe this one case, making it as comprehensible as possible. Its absolute historical accuracy is not important to us.

There was a woman with other guests at an evening party, a farewell party for the mistress of the house, who suffered from nervousness and was about to leave for a health resort abroad. She was to leave that evening. After the party had broken up and the hostess had departed, the woman whose case we are describing was walking with other guests along the street when a cab came around the corner behind them — not an automobile, but a cab with horses driven at a great pace. In smaller cities people returning home at night often walk in the middle of the street instead of on the sidewalk. (I do not know if you have noticed this.) As the cab rushed toward them, the guests scattered to the right and left and onto the sidewalks, with the exception of this one woman we are considering. She ran along the street in front of the horses, and all the driver's cursing and swearing and cracking of his whip could not make her move aside. She ran until she came to a bridge where she tried to throw herself into the water in order to avoid being run over. She was rescued by people on the bridge and returned to her party, thus being preserved from a serious accident.

This behavior was of course connected with the woman's general condition. It is undoubtedly due to hysteria when a person runs in the middle of the street in front of horses, and the cause of such behavior had to be discovered. In this and other cases, Freud began by looking for some of the causes in the patient's past — in childhood, or earlier life in general. If something had happened to the patient in the past that had not been completely assimilated by the soul, the event could leave behind an impulse to a certain behavior that could then be triggered later by any shocking experience.

And indeed such an experience was found in the childhood of the woman in question. As a child, she had been taken for a ride in a carriage, and the horses became frightened and ran away straight toward the river. The coachman jumped off and called to the girl to do the same. She jumped down at the last minute, just before horses and carriage plunged into the river. Then the later shocking incident occurred, and a certain association of horse with horse was there also. At the moment when she realized the danger from the horses, she lost control of herself, and ran frantically in front of them instead of turning aside — all this as an aftereffect of the childhood experience. You see that the psychoanalysts have a scientific method — at least according to present-day scientific ideas. But there are of course many people who have had some such experience in childhood without such a reaction; they would not run in front of the horses even if they associated them with horses from their past. To this one event something had to be added to lead to a "predisposition" to run in front of the horses, instead of stepping out of their way.

Freud continued his investigation, and actually found an interesting connection in this case. The woman who had run in front of the horses was engaged to be married, but was in love with two men at the same time. One was her fiancé, whom she was sure she loved best, but she also loved the other. So she was not quite clear about the matter, only halfway so. She also loved the other man, who was the husband of her best friend — the very friend whose farewell party had taken place that evening. The hostess, who had begun to suffer from nervousness, made her departure, and this woman left with the other guests, ran in front of the horses, was rescued, and was naturally brought back into the house she had just left. Further inquiry revealed that in the past there had existed a significant association between this lady and the husband of her best friend. The love affair had already taken on "certain dimensions," let us say, which accounted for the nervousness of her friend, as you can easily imagine. The physician brought her to this point in the story, but had difficulty in persuading her to continue. She admitted at last that when she came to herself in her friend's house, and was again normal, the husband declared his love to her. Quite a remarkable case, as you see!

Dr. Freud researched other, similar cases, and his findings convinced him that the hysterical symptoms, which had been attributed to a psychic trauma or wound, were due to love, whether conscious or unconscious. Freud believed that research into the patient's past, regardless of circumstances, would always reveal that love was playing its game in some way. Of course, these love stories have not necessarily risen into the patient's consciousness; indeed, in the most characteristic cases, they have not.

So Freud completed what he called his neurosis theory or sexual theory. He considered that sexuality entered into all such cases. But such things are extraordinarily tempting and tricky. First of all, in our time, we find everywhere an inclination to call on sex to explain any human problem. Thus it is not surprising that a doctor who found it to be a factor in so many cases of hysteria sets up such a theory.

On the other hand, this is the point where the greatest danger lies, because analytical psychology is carrying on research with inadequate tools. The matter is dangerous, first of all, because this longing for knowledge is so extremely tempting — tempting because of current circumstances and because it may always be proved that sexual relationships play a role. Yet the psychoanalyst Jung of Zurich, who wrote *Über die Psychologie des Unbewussten* ("On the Psychology of the Unconscious") does not share the opinion that Freud's sexual theory or neurosis theory is sufficient to explain such cases.[8] He has another theory.

Jung noted that Freud has opponents. Among them is a certain Adler, who takes a quite different viewpoint.[9] Freud examined numerous cases and found that the sexual factor played a role in each of them, and therefore settled upon sex as the original cause — you can read it all in Jung's book. But Adler approached the problem from another perspective, and decided that it was more important than the one Freud placed in the foreground.

Adler — I will put it only in general terms — found that there was another drive that played as important a role in the human being as the sexual one, namely, the drive for power, power over one's environment or power in general. According to Nietzsche, the "will to power" is supposedly a philosophical principle. And one can find as many cases to support the theory of the hunger for power as Freud found for his sexual theory.

One need only analyze patients suffering from hysteria; they are not at all rare. For example, imagine a woman is hysterical and has spasms — heart spasms are a favorite in such cases — as well as all sorts of other conditions. Her family and the whole household are stirred up, everything possible is done, doctors are summoned, and the patient is greatly pitied. In short, she exercises a tyrannical power over her environment. A reasonable person knows that there is usually nothing really wrong with the patient, even though she feels she is sick and suffers from it. Such patients are in reality perfectly healthy — but ill when they wish to be. You can diagnose them as both healthy and sick at the same time. Of course, they fall down when they faint in a heart spasm, but as a rule they fall on the rug, not on the bare floor! These things can be observed.

Now this unconscious drive for power leads very easily to hysterical conditions. Adler examined the cases at his disposal for this drive for power, and found that everywhere the hysterical symptoms appeared because the lust for power had somehow been aroused and distorted into pathological extremes. Jung said to himself: "Oh well, one cannot say Freud is wrong; what he observed is there. And one cannot say Adler is wrong; what he observed is also there. So it is probably sometimes one way, and sometimes the other!"

That is quite reasonable; it is indeed sometimes one way and sometimes another, but Jung built a special theory upon this. Jung's theory is not uninteresting if you do not take it abstractly, simply as a theory, but instead can see the impulses of our time at work in it, especially the feebleness of understanding in our age and its inadequacy. Jung says there are two types of people. In one type, feeling is more developed; in the other, thinking.

Here again, a great scholar made an "epoch-making" discovery, which actually every reasonable person can always easily make right in his or her immediate environment. After all, it is obvious that human beings can be divided into thinking people and feeling people. But erudition has a different task: it must not regard things as laypeople would and simply say that there are two types of people, feeling people and rationalists. Erudition or scholarship must add something, and it says in this case that the one who feels his way into things sends out his own force into the object. The other draws back from the object, or halts before it and reflects on it. The first is called the "extravert" type, the other the "introvert." The first would be the feeling person, the second the rationalist. These are scholarly categories, are they not? Ingenious, brilliant, really descriptive, at least up to a point — that is not to be denied!

Then Jung goes on to say: In the case of the extravert — that is, of the person who prefers to live in his or her feelings — the intellectual concepts very frequently remain stuck in the subconscious mind. Thus these people find themselves in a conflict between what is in their consciousness and the intellectual concepts teeming in their subconscious. And this conflict can lead to all kinds of conditions, characteristic primarily of people of this type.

In the case of rationalists, people in whom the mind predominates, the feelings remain down below, swarm in the subconscious, and come into collision with the conscious life, which cannot understand what is surging up, namely, the subconscious feelings. Because human beings are never finished and complete, but are sometimes this type and sometimes the other, circumstances may come about causing the subconscious mind to revolt against the conscious, and this can often lead to hysterical conditions.

Now we can say that Jung's theory is simply a paraphrase of the banal and trite division of people into feeling and rational types without adding anything to the facts. However, from all this you must realize that people of our time are at least beginning to notice all sorts of psychic peculiarities and are starting to ask what goes on within a person showing such symptoms. And they have at least advanced far enough to realize that these symptoms are not due to physiological or anatomical changes. People have already outgrown mere materialism in that they speak of psychic phenomena. So this is one way people try to emerge from materialism, and to reach some knowledge of the soul.

When you look at the subject more closely, however, you will see that people are led onto strange paths because the means they use to try to gain knowledge are so inadequate. But I must emphasize that these people do not realize onto what paths they are driven, and their supporters, readers, and contemporaries do not see it either. Thus, rightly seen, the whole thing has actually a very dangerous side, because so much is not taken into consideration, but instead rumbles around in people's subconscious. Strangely enough, it is the theories themselves that cause a commotion in people's subconscious. The researchers set up a theory about the subconscious, and with this they themselves agitate the subconscious.

Jung approaches the matter as a physician, and it is important that patients are treated psychologically and therapeutically from that standpoint. Many people are striving to introduce this matter into pedagogy and to apply it there. Thus we are no longer dealing merely with a limited theory, but with an effort to make it into a cultural influence. It is interesting to see how someone like Jung, who approaches this matter as a physician, and has studied, treated, and apparently even cured all sorts of cases, is driven further and further. According to him, when such abnormal psychological symptoms are found, one must search to discover any incidents in childhood that made an impression on the person's soul life and produced aftereffects. That is something especially sought for in this field: aftereffects of something that happened in childhood. I have mentioned an example that plays such a big role in the literature of psychoanalysis.

Then Jung found that in many cases of genuine illness one cannot prove that the patient as an individual is suffering from any such aftereffects no matter how far back into earliest childhood one goes. If you take into consideration everything the patient has come in contact with, you find the conflict within the individual, but no explanation of its cause. So Jung was led to distinguish *two* kinds of unconscious: first the *individual* unconscious, existing in each person but, of course, not on a conscious level. Thus if the young woman in her childhood jumped out of a carriage and received a shock, the incident has long since vanished from her conscious mind and works only subconsciously. If you consider this unconscious element (made up of innumerable details), you get the personal or individual unconscious. This is the first type Jung distinguished.

But the second is the suprapersonal or *collective* unconscious. According to Jung, there are things affecting the soul life that are neither in the individual personality nor in the outside world and therefore must be assumed to exist in a soul world.

The aim of psychoanalysis is to bring such soul contents into consciousness. That is supposed to be the healing method: to bring everything into consciousness. Thus the physician must try to extract from patients not only what they have experienced individually, but also what was neither an individual experience nor in the outside world but is contained in the soul. This led psychoanalysts to say that an individual experiences not only what he or she goes through after physical birth, but also all sorts of things from before birth, and all this then rumbles around inside the person. Thus people born today experience the Oedipus saga on a subconscious level. They do not just learn about it in school but "experience" it. They experience the Greek gods, the whole past of humanity. Unfortunately, however, these experiences want to come up into the conscious mind. Psychoanalysts must therefore say — and they do indeed go so far — that the children in ancient Greece also experienced this, but since they were told about it, they could experience it consciously. We nowadays also experience it, but it only rumbles around within us — for extraverts, in the subconscious thoughts, and for introverts in the subconscious feelings. These experiences simmer within people and rumble around in them like demons.

Now consider the necessity that confronts the psychoana-

lysts if they want to be true to their theory. They would necessarily have to take these things seriously and say simply
that if people may be made ill while growing up by their relationship to what simmers within them — a relationship of
which they know nothing — then this must be brought to
their consciousness. It must be explained to the patients that
there is a spiritual world inhabited by different gods. After
all, even psychoanalysts will admit that the human soul has a
connection to the gods, but they think the fact that the soul
knows nothing of this connection causes illness.

In their search for information and knowledge, psychoanalysts resort to all kinds of expedients, some of them quite
grotesque. Let us assume that a patient suffering from hysteria
needs to be treated for this or that symptom caused by fear of
a demon, a fire demon, let's say. In the past, people believed in
fire demons; they had visions of them and knew about them.
Nowadays people still have connections with them, as psychoanalysts will admit, but these connections are not conscious.
In addition, no one explains that there are fire demons, so
these unconscious relationships become a cause of illness.

Jung even goes so far as to assert that the gods, with whom
we are connected without knowing it, will become angry and
avenge themselves. Their revenge shows up as hysteria. Very
well, it amounts to this: In our time, individuals who are tormented in their subconscious mind by a demon do not know
that there are demons in fire. A fire demon torments them;
yet they cannot establish a relationship with him because that
would be superstition! What do these poor modern people do
when they become ill from all this? They project the matter
into the outer world, that is, they look up some friend they
had liked quite well and say: This is the one who persecutes

me and gripes about me! They feel persecuted, which means in fact that they have a demon tormenting them, but they have transferred it to another person.

In treating such a case, psychoanalysts often divert this transference to themselves. Thus, it often happens that patients make their doctor, for better or worse, into a god or a devil. So, you see, modern doctors perforce have to admit that people are tormented by spirits, but as they are taught nothing about such spirits, people cannot take possession of them in their conscious minds. As a result they pester and plague each other, projecting their demons onto each other, talking each other into all kinds of demoniacal nonsense, and so on.

And how disastrous psychoanalysts think this is can be seen from the following case Jung describes. He says that some of his colleagues claim that the soul energies resulting from such torment must be guided into other channels. Let us return then to one of the elementary cases of psychoanalysis. A female patient seeks treatment; her illness was caused, according to her psychoanalytical confession, by her having been in love many years ago with a man who rejected her. This had remained with her. Of course, maybe she is plagued by a demon, but in most cases coming to doctors' attention it turns out that something happened in the individual unconscious, which they distinguish from the collective unconscious. They try to redirect this immature fantasy or to transform it. If a love-starved soul can be persuaded to pour her unrequited love into humanitarian services, perhaps organizing this or that benefit, things may turn out well. But Jung himself says that it is not always possible to direct the energy in this way. Energies created in the soul in this way have a certain "gradient" that cannot be altered. Well, I have nothing against these expressions, but I would like to point out that they only circumscribe what laypeople often say in their own words. Jung describes a very interesting case that shows clearly that this gradient cannot be changed.

An American, a typical modern man, a self-made man, the efficient head of a business he had built up, had devoted himself to his work and achieved great success and wealth. Then he thought, "I will soon be forty-five and have done my bit! Now I will give myself a rest." So he decided to retire. He bought an estate with cars and tennis courts and everything else that goes with it. He intended to live in the country and simply to draw his percentage of the business profits. But when he had been on the estate for a while, he stopped playing tennis or driving his car or going to the theater. He no longer took pleasure in the gardens that were laid out, but sat in his room alone and brooded. He was hurting here and there; he had pain everywhere. First his head hurt, then his chest, and then his legs. He could not stand himself and no longer laughed, but instead was tired, weary, and always had a headache — it was terrible. The doctors could not diagnose any illness in the man. That happens with many people nowadays, does it not? They are perfectly healthy, and yet are ill.

Thus the doctor could only say that the man's trouble was psychic. He had adapted himself to the conditions in his business, and his energies would not readily adjust to another course. They follow their own gradient, which cannot be changed. So the doctor recommended that the man go back to business. The man in question understood the doctor's advice and followed it. But he found that he was no longer any good at business! He was just as ill there as at home.

From this Jung rightly concludes that you cannot easily transfer energy from one gradient to another, nor even turn it back again when you have failed in the attempt to redirect it. This man eventually came to him for treatment, but Jung could not help the American. It was already too late; the illness had spread too far and should have been treated earlier. You see from this that the therapy with transference is not without problems and difficulties, and Jung himself offers this example.

Everywhere we find important facts that can only be successfully dealt with, as I can now say, by spiritual science or spiritual psychology. These facts exist, and people notice them; the questions are there. It will be discovered that human beings are complicated, and not the simple creatures presented to us by nineteenth-century science.

Nowadays psychoanalysts are confronted by a peculiar fact that is completely inexplicable for modern science. Through spiritual psychology, with the means provided in my lectures, you will easily find an explanation. Of course, I can come back to the point at issue if you do not find the explanation by yourself. For example, it can happen that someone becomes blind due to hysteria; the blindness then is a symptom of hysteria. There are indeed such blind people who are physically able to see, yet do not; they are psychically blind. Now they are sometimes partially cured; that is, they begin to see again, but they do not see everything. In some cases the psychically blind people have recovered sufficient sight to see others, except that they do not see other people's heads. Such half-cured persons walk in the streets and see other people without heads. That can really happen; indeed there are even more curious things.

All this can be dealt with through spiritual psychology,

and in a lecture I gave here last year you can find the explanation for this inability to see the heads of other people.[10] Well, present-day psychoanalysts are confronted with all these symptoms. And they have seen enough to realize that it can be disastrous for people to have a relationship to the suprapersonal unconscious. But, for God's sake — actually, psychoanalysts do not say "for God's sake," but perhaps "for science's sake" — let us not take the spiritual world seriously! It does not enter their minds to take the spiritual world seriously, and this leads to something very peculiar. Few people notice the strange phenomena that appear as a result of these things. I want to point out a passage in Jung's recently published book *Über die Psychologie des Unbewussten* ("On the Psychology of the Unconscious") that will show you how far psychoanalysts are going nowadays.[11] I will have to read you that passage. Jung here presents examples showing that we have within us not only what is in our individual life or in the present, but also primordial connections to all sorts of demonic, divine, or spiritual forces, and so on.

Having shown, in this example, how new ideas arise out of the treasure-house of primordial images [here Jung does not call them gods but primordial images], we will proceed to the further discussion of the transference process. We saw that the libido had, for its new object, seized upon those seemingly absurd and singular fantasies, the contents of the collective unconscious. [The collective unconscious is the suprapersonal unconscious, not the personal.] As I have already said, the projection of primordial images upon the doctor is a danger not to be underrated at this stage of the treatment. [The patient projects his or her demons onto the doctor. That is a danger.] The images contain not only all the fine and good things that humanity has ever thought and felt, but the worst infamies and devilries of which men have been capable.[12]

Just think! Jung has reached the point of understanding that human beings have unconsciously within them all the most fiendish crimes as well as the most beautiful things that humanity has ever been able to think and feel. These people cannot be persuaded to speak of Lucifer and Ahriman, but they agree upon a statement like this:[13]

The images contain not only all the fine and good things that humanity has ever thought and felt, but the worst infamies and devilries of which men have been capable. . . . Now if the patient is unable to distinguish the personality of the doctor from these projections, all hope of an understanding is finally lost and a human relationship becomes impossible. But if the patient avoids this Charybdis, he is wrecked on the Scylla of *introjecting* these images — in other words, he ascribes their peculiarities not to the doctor but to himself. [Then the patient is the devil.] This is just as disastrous. In projection, he vacillates between an extravagant and pathological deification of the doctor, and a contempt bristling with hatred. In introjection, he gets involved in a ridiculous self-deification, or else a moral self-laceration. The mistake he makes in both cases comes from attributing to a *person* the contents of the collective unconscious. In this way he makes himself or his partner either god or devil. . . . This is the reason why men have always needed demons and cannot live without gods, except for a few particularly clever specimens of *homo occidentalis* who lived yesterday or the day before, supermen whose "god is dead" because they themselves have become gods — but tin gods with thick skulls and cold hearts. [14]

You see, psychoanalysts arrive necessarily at the conclusion that the human soul is so constituted that it needs gods, that gods are necessary to it, for the soul becomes ill without them. Therefore, the soul has always had gods; human beings need gods. Psychoanalysts even mock people by saying that when we lack gods, we make gods of ourselves, but only "tin gods with thick skulls and cold hearts." They go on to say, "The idea of God is an absolutely necessary psychological function of an irrational nature. . . . "

To describe the necessity of the concept of God like this in a scientific way is as far as one can go. Human beings must have God; they need Him, as psychoanalysts know. But that sentence does not end there; let me read you how it ends. "The idea of God is an absolutely necessary psychological function of an irrational nature, which has nothing whatever to do with the question of God's existence."

When you read the complete sentence, you come upon the great dilemma of our time. Psychoanalysts can prove to you that people become ill if they have no God, but they claim this need for God has nothing to do with the existence or nonexistence of God. Jung continues:

For this question [whether God exists] is one of the most stupid questions one can pose.[15] . . . Our intellect has long known that we can form no proper idea of God, much less picture to ourselves in what manner he really exists, if at all.[16]

Now I ask you, are we not at a point here where we can see

things very clearly? These things are there, knocking on the doors of knowledge. People who are seeking are also there; they admit an absolute necessity, but when that necessity is posed as a serious question, they consider it one of the stupidest that can be asked.

You have here one of the points in present-day cultural life where you can see exactly what is usually ignored. I can assure you that in terms of their knowledge and study of the soul these psychoanalysts are far ahead of what psychiatry and psychology currently offer in the universities. Indeed, in a certain sense, they are right to look down upon those dreadful so-called sciences. But one can catch them in such a passage that shows what humanity is actually confronted with in contemporary science.

Many people are not aware of this. They do not realize how strong trust in authority is nowadays. There has never been such trust in authority, nor has it ever been so completely unconscious as it is today. One cannot help but asking again and again just what therapists do to treat cases of hysteria. They look for a content in the subconscious mind that has not been resolved in the person's conscious. Yes, but you find plenty of such unconscious material in the theorists themselves. When you lift it into full consciousness, it turns out to be exactly what you are becoming conscious of right now and what has been simmering in the unconscious of modern doctors and their patients. And all our literature is so saturated with this unconscious content that you are daily and hourly exposed to the danger of absorbing it. And since it is only through spiritual psychology that people can become aware of these things, many take in such material unknowingly and absorb it into their unconscious where it then remains.

At least, psychoanalysts have made us aware that the reality of the soul is to be accepted as such. They have done that. But the devil is at their heels. By that I mean that they are neither able nor willing to approach spiritual reality. Therefore we find everywhere the most incredible statements. But people in our time do not pay enough attention to perceive these things. We naturally expect any reader of Jung's book to fall off his chair at such sentences, but people of our time do not do that. Just think how much must be in the unconscious of modern humanity. And because psychoanalysts see how much there is in the unconscious — and this they do see — they see many things differently than other people. In the preface to his book, for example, Jung says something that is, at least in part, not bad.

The psychological accompaniments of the present war — above all the incredible brutalization of common judgments, the mutual slanderings, the unprecedented fury of destruction, the unheard-of lying, and the inability of men to call a halt to the bloody demon — are uniquely fitted to force upon the attention of every thinking person the problem of the chaotic unconscious which slumbers uneasily beneath the ordered world of consciousness. This war has pitilessly revealed to civilized man that he is still a barbarian, and has at the same time shown what an iron scourge lies in store for him if ever again he should be tempted to make his neighbors responsible for his own evil qualities. The psychology of the individual is reflected in the psychology of the nation.[17]

And now comes a sentence that makes you wonder what to do with it.

What the nation does is done also by each individual, and so long as the individual continues to do it, the nation will do likewise. Only a change in the attitude of the individual can initiate a change in the psychology of the nation.

These sentences, placed side by side, clearly have a destructive effect on thinking. I would like to ask you if it makes any sense to say: "What the nation does is done also by each individual"? If it did, it would also have to be reasonable to ask: Could each individual do it without the nation's doing it too? It is nonsense, is it not, to say things like that. And it is such nonsense that seems to impress and overwhelm even great and prominent thinkers these days. And this sort of thinking is not only to become therapy, but to provide guidelines for pedagogy. This again is founded upon the justifiable longing to introduce into pedagogy a new soul and spiritual element. However, should conclusions be introduced into pedagogy that were reached with entirely inadequate methods? These are the important questions of our time.

We will return to the matter from the standpoint of spiritual psychology and illuminate it from a larger perspective. Then we will see that to do justice to these things at all, we must grasp them in a much larger context. But they must also be dealt with concretely. Above all, these problems, which are still being investigated only with the old, inadequate methods, must be placed in the light of the knowledge of spiritual psychology.

Take, for example, the problem of Nietzsche.[18] Today I can only outline it; tomorrow we can consider such problems more thoroughly. As we know already from earlier lectures, from 1841 to 1879, there was the battle of spirits above; from 1879 on, we have the fallen spirits in the human realm.[19] In future, such things and others like them must of necessity play a role in studying a human life. Nietzsche was born in 1844; for three years before he descended to earth his soul was in the spiritual realm in the midst of the spiritual battle. During his boyhood Schopenhauer was still living, but died in 1860.[20] Only after Schopenhauer's death did Nietzsche devote himself to the study of his writings. The soul of Schopenhauer cooperated from the spiritual worlds above. That was the real relationship. Nietzsche was reading Schopenhauer, and while he was absorbing the latter's writings, Schopenhauer was working upon Nietzsche's thoughts.

What was Schopenhauer's situation in the spiritual realm? From 1860 on, through the years when Nietzsche was reading his books, Schopenhauer was in the midst of the spiritual battle that was still being fought on that plane. Therefore Schopenhauer's inspiration of Nietzsche was colored by what he had gathered from the battle of spirits in which he was involved. In 1879, these spirits were cast down from heaven onto the earth. Up to 1879 Nietzsche's spiritual development followed very curious paths. They will be explained in the future as resulting from the influence of Schopenhauer and Wagner.[21] In my book *Friedrich Nietzsche: A Fighter for Freedom,* you can find many indications supporting this.[22] Up to that time, Wagner had had no particular influence except that he was active on earth. Wagner was born in 1813; the battle of the spirits only began in 1841. But Wagner died in 1883, and Nietzsche's spiritual development took a peculiar turn when Wagner's influence began. Wagner entered the spiritual world in 1883, when the battle of spirits was already over, and the defeated spirits had been cast to earth. Nietzsche was in the midst of things here when the spirits began to roam the earth, while Wagner lived in the spiritual realm after those spirits had already been expelled. Wagner's influence upon Nietzsche after the former's death had an entirely different objective than that of Schopenhauer.

This is where the concrete though suprapersonal influences begin, not those abstract demonic ones of which the psychoanalysts speak. Humanity will have to resolve to enter this concrete spiritual world and to comprehend things that are obvious when the facts are checked. In the future, Nietzsche's biography will be based on the fact that he was inspired by Richard Wagner, who was born in 1813 and who participated in everything that led to the brilliant man whose development up to 1879 I described in my book. Such a biography will also explain that Nietzsche was influenced by Schopenhauer from his sixteenth year on, when Schopenhauer was involved in the spiritual battle fought on the spiritual plane before 1879. It will show that Nietzsche was exposed to Wagner's influence after the latter had died and entered the spiritual world, while Nietzsche himself was still here below, where the spirits of darkness were at work.

Jung considers this a fact: Nietzsche found a demon, and projected it upon Wagner. Oh well — projections, gradients, introvert or extravert human types —- all these are words for abstractions, but they say nothing about realities! These things are truly important. We are not agitating for a world view we have adopted. Rather everything *outside* of this world-view shows how much present-day humanity needs this view!

LECTURE TWO
PSYCHOANALYSIS AND SPIRITUAL PSYCHOLOGY II
November 11, 1917

Y ESTERDAY I DESCRIBED what is called "analytical psychology" or "psychoanalysis" as an effort to gain knowledge about the soul by inadequate means. Perhaps nothing is as well-suited as psychoanalysis to show that in our time everything urges us toward spiritual psychology. Yet, at the same time, people resist a spiritually scientific consideration of reality because of their unconscious prejudices. Yesterday I gave you examples of the grotesque leaps the thinking of our modern erudition necessarily makes when it dares to approach soul problems. And I showed you how to catch modern scholars at these leaps in their reasoning. I pointed out that one of the better psychoanalysts, C.G. Jung, categorizes people as belonging either to the predominantly thinking type or to the predominantly feeling type. On that basis he assumed that in people of the thinking type, unconscious feeling impulses rush up against the thinking in the conscious mind and thus lead to soul conflicts. In the other type, Jung assumed thoughts from the unconscious mind rush up against the feeling life and cause soul conflicts.

Now you might say that these things will be fought out in scientific discussions and that we can wait until people make up their minds to overcome their unconscious prejudice against spiritual psychology. But passive waiting becomes impossible when such things do not confine themselves to the theoretical field, but are encroaching upon practical life and cultural development. And psychoanalysis is not content to limit itself to therapy alone, which might be less alarming since there seems to be little difference — I said *seems* to be — between it and other therapeutic methods. Instead it is trying to extend itself to pedagogy and to become the foundation of a pedagogical approach. This makes it necessary for us to point out the dangers in quarter-truths more emphatically and more seriously than would be called for by a mere theoretical discussion.

To discuss this matter fully will take quite some time, but today we can begin by enlarging the scope of our consideration and casting light on one or the other of its aspects. First of all, I would like to point out that the facts available to psychoanalysts are really suited to lead them to a spiritual realm modern people do not wish to enter, at least not in an accurate manner. Rather they would prefer to leave it as a sort of nebulous, unconscious region, for our current outlook, ailing with materialism even in this domain, loves nothing more than a vague, mystical floating among all sorts of unexplained, undefined concepts. We find the most grotesque, the most repulsive mysticism right in the midst of materialism, if you take mysticism to mean a floating about in all sorts of nebulous ideas, without working out one's worldview into clear, sharply defined concepts. The contents of soul life push the psychoanalysts into the domain of extraconscious intelligence and reasoning activity. I have often dealt with these matters — only indicating them and without going into details, since they are taken for granted by students of spiritual psychology. In the process I have often reminded you that reasoning, intellectual activity, or cleverness are not confined to human consciousness, but are everywhere, that we are surrounded by effective mental activity as we are surrounded by air. Rational activity surrounds us and all other beings like a cocoon.

The facts available to the psychoanalysts might easily lead them to this insight. Yesterday I cited a case described by Jung. It had to do with a woman who, having left an evening party with other guests, was frightened by horses, and ran in front of them along the street to the river where she was rescued. She was brought back to the house she had left, where her host declared his love for her. From the standpoint of Freud or Adler the case is easily explained on the basis of the drive for love or power, but this diagnosis does not touch the vital, essential foundation of the matter. Its foundation is reached only by realizing that consciousness is more than the cleverness and calculation, the cunning and craftiness of what works in us as intellect, and by realizing that the laws of life are not limited by the laws of consciousness.

In the case we have discussed, we can at least ask what the woman really wanted after she had been at the party and had seen her friend depart for the health resort. She wanted to create the opportunity for what actually happened, namely, to be alone with her friend's husband. Of course this had nothing to do with what was in her consciousness, what she was aware of and would have owned up to. It would not have been proper, as we say. Something had to be brought about that she would not have to own up to. We will find the true explanation by taking into account her subconscious, cunning intellect, of which she herself was unaware. Throughout the entire evening she had wanted to be alone with her host. People who are not so clever make a poor choice of means to reach their objective, but those who are cleverer make a better choice. In this case, we can say that in the woman's ordinary consciousness, which admitted scruples as to what was proper or improper, allowed or not allowed, the effective and direct means to achieve the end in view could not have been chosen. But in what was stored below the layer of ordinary consciousness, this thought was incessantly active: "I must manage a meeting alone with the man. I must make use of the next opportunity that presents itself to return to the house."

We can say that if the opportunity with the horses had not offered itself, supported by association with the earlier accident, she would have found some other excuse; for example, she could have fainted in the street. We can say with a kind of hypothetical certainty that the woman would surely have fainted if the approaching cab had not provided the opportunity she needed. She would have fainted on the street, and people would have carried her back to the house she had just left. If she had not fainted, then she would have found some other expedient. The unconscious ignores all the scruples the conscious mind cannot disregard. The unconscious takes the attitude that "the end justifies the means," whether they harmonize with our ideas of propriety and morality or not.

In such a case we are reminded of what Nietzsche, who knew something about many of these things, called the *great* reason in contrast to the *small* reason. The great reason is the all-inclusive reason that does not come into consciousness, but acts below the threshold of consciousness and leads people to do many things to which they do not own up in their conscious minds. Through the ordinary, outer consciousness, human beings are connected with the world of the senses, the whole physical world, and all that lives in it. To this physical world also belong all the concepts of propriety, of bourgeois morality, and so forth. All of this is part of the physical plane, and human beings are equipped with a consciousness relating them to that plane.

In our unconscious, however, we are connected with an entirely different world, which Jung says the soul needs because it is related to that world; but he also says that it is foolish to inquire about the real existence of that world. Well, that is how it is: as soon as the threshold of consciousness is crossed, the human soul is no longer in a merely material context or environment, but in a realm where thoughts rule that may be very cunning.

Jung is correct in saying that especially people of our time, the so-called people of culture, need to pay attention to these things. For this so-called contemporary culture has the peculiarity of pressing numerous impulses down into the unconscious, impulses that then assert themselves in such a way that irrational behavior, as it is called, and irrational conduct result. When the drive for power or love is mentioned, it is because as soon as the human soul enters the unconscious regions, it approaches the realm where these drives rule. It is not these drives themselves that cause the irrational behavior, but the fact that the person plunges with his or her unconscious intelligence into regions where these drives are in effect.

The woman in our case would not have gone to such great lengths and involved her unconscious cunning for anything that interested her less than her love affair. She had to have a special interest in the matter. And that the love impulse so often plays an important role is simply because the love interest is so very common and widespread. If psychoanalysts did not focus so much on psychoanalytic sanatoriums, where the majority of the patients, it seems to me, are women — the same reproach is cast on anthroposophical events but, I think, with less justification — if psychoanalysts were more experienced in other fields, as some of them are, and if there were a greater variety of cases in the sanatoriums, they might gain more extensive knowledge.

Let us assume that a sanatorium was established especially for psychiatric treatment of people who had become nervous or hysterical from playing the stock market. Then one could introduce quite different things into the unconscious on the same basis that Freud introduced the love impulse. Then we could see the extensive, unconscious cunning processes of the people who play the stock market. Then, through the usual methods of elimination, sexual love would be seen to play a very small part, and yet the subtleties of unconscious cunning and slyness could be studied at their height. Even the drive for power could not always be designated as the primary impulse, but altogether different drives would be found ruling the regions into which our soul descends when we enter the realm of the unconscious.

If in addition a sanatorium were established for scholars suffering from hysteria, it would be found that what works in their unconscious can rarely be traced back to the drive for love. For those with any knowledge in this field realize that under present conditions scholars are seldom drawn to their chosen science by love, but by quite different forces that would be revealed if brought to the surface through psycho-analysis. The all-embracing truth is that the soul is led from the realm of the conscious down into the unconscious regions — which can become conscious only with the help of spiritual science — where our drives and instincts rule. These drives cannot be mastered because we can conquer only what is in our conscious mind. There we have another inconvenient truth! Of course, it forces people to realize that in their unconscious mind human beings can be very sly creatures and much more cunning than they are in their ordinary conscious mind — more cunning than even the psychoanalysts are prepared to admit. In this field we can have some strange experiences with ordinary science. You can read about these experiences in the second chapter of my new book *Von Seelenrätseln* ("Riddles of the Soul"), which will be published soon.[1] In that section I deal with what the academic Dessoir dared to write in the chapter on anthroposophy in his book *Vom Jenseits der Seele* ("Beyond the Limits of the Soul").[2] This second chapter of my *Von Seelenrätseln* will be useful for thinking people who want to form an opinion about the morality of present-day scholars. You will see when you read this chapter what kind of opposition we are dealing with. Of the points mentioned in my book, I will here bring up only a few that are related to our present theme.

Dessoir has all sorts of objections to this and that and always refers to passages taken from my books. In a very interesting context he tells how I distinguish consecutive cultural periods: the Indian, the ancient Persian, the Chaldean-Egyptian, the Greco-Latin, and now we live in the sixth, he says, "according to Steiner."

This proves that we have to refute these statements in a schoolmasterly manner, for it shows us the way to confront such an individual. How does Max Dessoir come to assert, in the midst of all his other nonsense, that I said we are living in the sixth post-Atlantean cultural epoch? It may be easily explained if you have any practice in philological methods. I worked for six and a half years at the Goethe Archives in Weimar and learned a little about how to use philological methods. So I can easily show through these methods how Dessoir came to attribute to me this statement regarding the sixth cultural epoch. He had been reading my book *An Outline of Esoteric Science,* in which there is a sentence leading to a description of our current fifth post-Atlantean cultural period.[3] In this sentence I say that things are prepared over long periods of time, and in one paragraph I explain that events taking place in the fourteenth and fifteenth centuries were prepared in the fourth, fifth, and sixth centuries.

About five lines further on, I say that the sixth century was a preparation for the fifth cultural period. Dessoir, as is typical of him, read only superficially and later checked hastily, as many a scholar does, the place he had highlighted in the margin with a red or black pencil, and confused what was said about the cultural period with what had been stated earlier about the fourth, fifth, and sixth centuries. Thus, he speaks of the "sixth cultural period" instead of the fifth because he had skipped a few lines.

You see the grand superficiality such a person works with. Here we have an example of how such "scholarship" may be shown up philologically. This entire chapter in his miserable concoction is riddled with such mistakes. And while Dessoir claims to have studied a number of my writings, I could prove philologically what books this number comprises. He read — and partly understood — *The Philosophy of Spiritual Activity,* for he devotes a sentence to it that is utter nonsense.[4] And he read *An Outline of Esoteric Science,* but in such a way as to end up with the kind of stuff I have just described. In addition, he read the small work *The Spiritual Guidance of Man,* and the little booklets *Reincarnation and Karma,* and *Blood Is a Very Special Fluid.*[5] This is all he read, as is clear from his essay. He read nothing else. That is the morality of our present-day scholars. It is important to expose the erudition of our time in such a context. Out of the great number of my books, he chose such a very small amount to read, and then he bases his whole argument on them — and with distorted thinking to boot. Many of our scholars these days do exactly the same thing. When they write about animals, for example, they usually have about as much material to base their observations on as Dessoir had.

Quite a pretty chapter could be written if we studied Max Dessoir's unconscious mind. He himself, however, in a special passage in his book, provides the opportunity for us to take his unconscious into account. Grotesquely enough, he relates that when he is lecturing, it sometimes happens that his thoughts go on even though his soul is no longer present with them. He thus continues to speak for a while, until he realizes from the reaction of his audience that his thoughts have gone in one direction and his attention in another. He tells this quite naïvely. Just think, on that basis he then proceeds to discuss all kinds of peculiarities of human consciousness. I have pointed out quite gently that Dessoir here reveals himself. At first I thought he could not possibly mean himself. He must simply identify with other, clumsy lecturers, and therefore he speaks in the first person. It would be unreasonable to think that he is describing himself. But he really does exactly that. In the discussion of such matters many odd things will be noted.

He deals with *The Philosophy of Spiritual Activity* in one comment, by formulating a trivial sentence that is Dessoirish and did not originate with me. The whole thing is crazy. He says in that passage, "Steiner's first book, *The Philosophy of Spiritual Activity.*" Well, since that book is the culmination of ten years' writing activity, I have to draw your attention to this spouting of academic paranoia, to such academic madness as an example of many scholars' ethics. I know of course that although I have shown in my book that Dessoir's presentation is corrupt, people will say again and again that Dessoir has refuted Steiner. I know it very well. Trying to break through what people nowadays imagine they have long since got completely rid of, namely, belief in authority — it is like talking to the wall.

But this chapter in Dessoir's book in particular will prove the difficulties spiritual psychology must struggle against in contemporary culture simply because it insists on clear, sharply defined concepts and concrete spiritual experiences. There is no question of logic with such an individual as Dessoir, and a lack of logic in the broadest sense characterizes our contemporary so-called scientific literature.

These are the reasons why official erudition and official spiritual trends, even if they work themselves out of such extreme inferiority as the psychiatry or psychology taught in the universities, will nevertheless never get anywhere. They lack the basic requirement, namely, a genuine observation of life. So long as it is not widely realized how far from genuine research and from a true sense for reality those things are that pose nowadays as scientific literature — I do not say, as science, but as scientific literature — and that often form the content of university lectures and popular talks, so long as this trust in authority is not broken, nothing good will come of it. These things must be said even if we have the deepest respect for scientific thinking and for the great achievements of natural science. That these things influence life in such contradictory fashion must be realized.

After this digression let us return to our subject. Dessoir

finds it especially aggravating that, as he maintains in a combination of objective untruth and slander, I said in my little book *The Spiritual Guidance of Man* that there is an important, unconscious working of spiritual impulses. I pointed them out by showing that while a child builds up his or her brain, a greater wisdom is at work than the one we later become conscious of when the brain is completed. A healthy science ought to take its starting point from such normal workings of the unconscious, but it would still need something else.

When you read my book *How to Know Higher Worlds,* you will find there a discussion of the secret of the threshold.[6] In my explanation of this secret, I show that after we cross the threshold into the spiritual world a kind of separation takes place, a sort of differentiation of the three fundamental powers of the soul: thinking, feeling, and willing. Remember that in that same book I explained in the description of the guardian of the threshold that these three forces, which work so closely together in ordinary consciousness that they can hardly be separated, now become independent of each other. If I sketch them, this narrow middle section (see drawing) is the boundary between the ordinary consciousness and that region where the soul lives in the spiritual world. Thinking, feeling, and willing must be so drawn as to show *this* as the range of will (red), but bordering upon the realm of feeling (green), and this in turn borders upon the realm of thinking (yellow). But if I were to sketch their paths after crossing the threshold into the spiritual world, I would have to show that thinking (yellow) becomes independent on the one hand; feeling (green, right) separates itself from thinking, and will becomes independent too (red, right). In other words, thinking, feeling, and willing spread out like a fan.

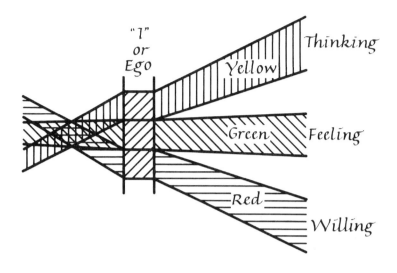

You will find this described in more detail in my book *How to Know Higher Worlds.* It is only because the threshold has a certain breadth in which our I lives that these three activities can interact properly and without getting confused. When our I is healthy, when it has perfect soul health, then the interaction of thinking, feeling, and willing is so regulated that they do not merge but only mutually influence each other. This is the essential secret of our I: it keeps thinking, feeling, and willing side by side so that they affect each other in the right way, but do not merge. Once we cross the threshold into the spiritual world, there is no danger of such a merging because then the three faculties separate.

Certain philosophers, such as Wundt, for example, insist that the soul must not be described as threefold because it is a unity.[7] Wundt too confuses everything. The fact is that in the spiritual world thinking, feeling, and willing originate in a threefold manner, yet in the soul on earth they act as a unity. That must be taken into consideration. When people claim, as they have recently done, that spiritual psychology distinguishes actually three souls even though there is only one, and that therefore there is no justification for spiritual psychology, then we must point out that the unity of the human being is not impaired by the fact that each of us has two hands.

The drawing on the previous page shows the relationship between the soul forces working in and with the I, as well as the way they work on the other side of the threshold of consciousness, in the spiritual world. However, a different condition can come about if the I has been weakened in any way. Then the threshold is crossed, as it were, in the opposite direction (see drawing, left). Then thinking swerves aside (yellow, left), mingles with feeling (green, left), and willing (red, left), and confusion results. This happens when thinking is in any danger of not being properly confined, so that it asserts itself autonomously in the conscious mind. Then, because the I is not working as it should, thinking slides into the sphere of feeling or of will. Instead of working side by side, thinking merges with feeling, or will, because the I is for some reason unable to exert its normal control.

This is what has happened in the cases categorized by the psychoanalysts as hysteria or nervousness. Thinking, feeling, and willing have swung to the opposite side, away from the healthy direction that would lead them into the spiritual realm. If you have any gift for testing this, you can easily see how it develops. Take the case of the woman sitting by her father's sickbed. Her formerly strong I-consciousness had been diminished through loss of sleep. The slightest thing might cause her thoughts to leave their track alongside her feelings and fall into them. Then the thoughts would at once be submerged in the waves of feeling, which are far stronger than the wave of thought, and the result in such a case is that the whole organism is seized by waves of feeling. This happens the moment thinking is no longer strong enough to hold itself apart from feeling.

It is an important demand placed on human beings that they learn more and more to hold their thinking apart from the waves of feeling and will. If thinking takes hold of the waves of feeling in the unconscious, something abnormal results in the organism. (See drawing: at the right is the supraconscious, in the middle the conscious, at the left the unconscious). This is extremely important.

Now you can imagine that in our modern life, when people are confronted with so many things they do not properly understand and cannot really penetrate, thoughts continually run over into feelings. However, only thinking is oriented on the physical plane; feeling is no longer confined to the physical plane but by its very nature is connected with the spiritual plane as well. Feeling really has a connection with all the spiritual beings who must be considered real. So that if a person with inadequate concepts sinks into his or her feeling life, he or she comes into collision with the gods — if you like to put it that way — but also with evil gods. And all these collisions occur because the person entered this realm without any reliable means of knowledge. Entering the feeling life without adequate means of knowledge is unavoidable when there is more going on in the sphere of feelings than in that of ordinary reason. In the sphere of feelings, human beings cannot liberate themselves from their connection with the spiritual world. When they free themselves in the realm of the intellect in this materialistic age, they enter the world of feeling with inadequate concepts and consequently must become ill.

What then is the only remedy to really restore people to health? They must be guided to concepts that reach out to include the world of feelings; that is to say, modern people must again be told of the spiritual world in the most comprehensive sense. The therapeutic methods of the psychoanalysts, which are adapted to the individual, are not what is needed, but rather spiritual science, which applies to all humanity. If people really take in the concepts of spiritual science — and not everyone who listens to lectures or reads about them really takes them in — if people really absorb them, it will not be possible for thinking, feeling, and willing to intermingle chaotically in the unconscious. This chaotic intermingling is at the root of hysteria and nervousness, which are psychological symptoms and are the subject of psychoanalysis.

However, all this requires that we have the courage to approach a direct experience of the concrete working of the spiritual worlds, the courage to realize that we are living now in a crisis connected with the one we have found in the year 1879, whose painful aftermath we are still suffering. I told you yesterday that many things must be looked at differently than the materialistic outlook of our time does, and I referred to Nietzsche as an example of this.

Nietzsche was born in 1844. In 1841, the battle in the spiritual world began, of which I have already spoken, and for three years Nietzsche was in the midst of it. Richard Wagner, born in 1813, at first took no part in it. So Nietzsche lived in the spiritual world for three years after the battle had begun. He absorbed all the impulses he could under the influence of this battle and brought them down to earth with him. If you read Nietzsche's early writings, you will notice his pugnacity. Almost every sentence shows the aftereffects of what he experienced spiritually in the three years from 1841 to 1844. This gave a definite coloring to all the writings of Nietzsche's early period.

As I have pointed out, another important event was that Schopenhauer died when Nietzsche was a boy of sixteen. Nietzsche then began reading Schopenhauer's works. A real relationship developed between the soul of Schopenhauer in the spiritual world and that of Nietzsche on earth. Nietzsche read every phrase of Schopenhauer so receptively that the author's impulses from the spiritual world could enter into him. Schopenhauer had ascended into the spiritual world in 1860 when the battle was still raging. What was his objective, what did he want? Under the influence of the battle, Schopenhauer wanted to see his thoughts rather than his works continue into the future. Nietzsche did indeed continue Schopenhauer's thoughts, but in a peculiar way. After passing through the gate of death, Schopenhauer saw that he had composed his writings in an epoch when the spirits of darkness were approaching but had not yet arrived on earth. Thus he wanted to have his thoughts and the impulses growing out of them continued into the future. That is, as he was confronted by the battle of the spirits of light against those of darkness in the spiritual world, Schopenhauer wanted to have his writings continued. He formed in Nietzsche's soul the impulses to continue his thoughts. What Nietzsche's soul received from the spiritual world at that time contrasted sharply with what was happening on the physical plane in his personal relationship with Richard Wagner. This is how Nietzsche's soul life as well as his career as a writer developed.

Then came the year 1879. The battle that had been raging in the spiritual realms began to be transferred to earth after the spirits of darkness had been flung down. Nietzsche's whole karma, in which I include his concrete relationship to the spiritual world, exposed him to the danger of being driven into very evil paths by the spirits of darkness. Schopenhauer had, as it were, a transcendent egoistic motivation. His soul was in the spiritual world and inspired Nietzsche to carry on his work. This is a transcendent egoistic motivation lasting beyond death. After all, egoism is not necessarily always bad.

But when Wagner entered the spiritual world in 1883, the spirits of darkness had already come down. Thus he entered into an entirely different atmosphere, so to speak. He became Nietzsche's unselfish spiritual guide — we have to speak about things here that are paradoxical but are nevertheless true. Wagner did not make Nietzsche carry on his work, but allowed him to remain in the current appropriate for him. And Wagner did Nietzsche the favor of letting him become mentally deranged at the right moment to keep him from getting into dangerous regions with his conscious mind. That sounds paradoxical, but this is how unselfishly Wagner's soul worked upon Nietzsche from realms that were purer than those where Schopenhauer's soul had acted, who had still been in the midst of the battle between the spirits of darkness and the spirits of light. What Wagner wanted to do for Nietzsche was to protect him in his karma, as far as possible, from the spirits of darkness, which had already descended to earth.

And indeed Nietzsche was protected from these spirits to a great extent. If you read his last writings in the right spirit, you will find great thoughts there, especially if you separate out the strong resistances or the things that have developed out of them. In my book *Nietzsche: A Fighter for Freedom,* I tried to show the mighty thought impulses detached from all his conflicting impulses.

Yes, "the world is deep." There is really some truth in Nietzsche's saying: "The world is deep, and deeper than the day divines." So we must not criticize the vast regions of the spiritual life with our ordinary consciousness. The wise guidance of the world can be understood only if we can enter into concrete aspects of that guidance while staying free of egoistic thoughts and if we can see even tragic events in the development of the world as part of the wisdom-filled course of things. If you really want to look into the heart of things, you will come upon many uncomfortable places.

In the future, if people really want to understand a life like Nietzsche's, they will not get anywhere by describing only what happened in his environment here on earth. Our view of life must be extended to include the spiritual world. This need to extend our view of life is made more than obvious by the phenomena the psychoanalysts face today and try in vain to master with inadequate means of knowledge. Society would be drifting into difficult situations if it accepted and complied with psychoanalysis, particularly in the field of pedagogy.

Why is this so? Consider the fact that thinking slips down into the sphere of feeling. As soon as we live with our soul in the sphere of feeling, we are no longer in the life limited by birth and death, or by conception and death. Instead we then live in the whole world, which extends beyond the usual lifespan (see drawing, A). In the realm of feelings, we live also in the period between our last death and our birth into this present life (B), and with our will we live even in our previous incarnation (C).

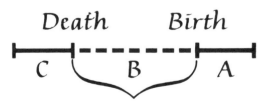

Imagine educators trying to work on the basis of psychoanalysis and their relationship with their students or patients. In trying to deal with soul content that has slipped down into the realm of feeling, such an educator approaches not only the individual life, but the all-embracing life extending far beyond the individual. Concerning this all-encompassing life, however, the connections between people cannot be exhaustively described by means of mere ideas but must lead instead into genuine life connections. This is very important. Imagine such a connection between a psychoanalytic teacher and a student. What would take place there could not be confined to the realm of ideas being conveyed to the student, but real karmic connections would have to be established because one is intervening much more deeply in life. In such a case, the individual in question would be torn out of his or her karma; the course of his or her karma would be changed. It will not do to deal with what extends beyond the individual in a purely individual manner. Instead it must be treated in a universally human way. We have all been brought together in a certain time period, so there must be a common element that acts as soon as we go beyond the individual. In other words, individuals cannot be approached in therapy or education by individuals, as psychoanalysts do, but something universal must enter. Even into the general culture of the times something must enter that points the soul to what usually remains in the unconscious. And what is brought up into consciousness must become part of the milieu, not a transaction between individuals.

Here, you see, lies the great mistake; it is a far-reaching and tremendously significant mistake. Instead of trying to permeate cultural life with knowledge of the spiritual world, as it should be in our times, the psychoanalysts shut all the souls that show how repressed spiritual life becomes pathological into sanatoriums and treat each one individually. This can only lead to the forming of confused karmic connections. What takes place between the individuals does not result in bringing to light the unconscious soul content, but creates a karmic bond between doctor and patient because it encroaches upon the individual.

This leads us into real, concrete life, and we must not play with that. Real, concrete life can only be mastered by striving for what is universally human. These things must be learned from the concrete relationships of human beings to the spiritual world. Therefore it would be good if people could stop talking abstractly, as Jung does, saying that the individual experiences everything humanity has gone through, even all sorts of demons. But Jung makes them into abstract demons, not realities, by saying that it is stupid to discuss whether they exist. He makes them into abstract demons, mere thought-demons that could never make anyone ill and that could never live in the unconscious but only in the conscious mind. That is the point: the people who accept such theories are themselves working with so many unconscious ideas that they can never come up with the right thing. Instead they end up making certain concepts absolute. And I have to repeat again that when we begin to make ideas absolute, then we come to a dead end, or we reach a pit and fall into it without thinking.

A man like Dr. Freud is obliged to extend the sexual domain over the entire human being in order to make it account for every soul phenomenon. Various people have approached me with psychoanalytic tendencies; I have said to them that a theory or worldview must hold its own when you apply it to itself, otherwise it crumbles into nothingness. The simple logical fallacy, if you extend it far enough, is an example. A Cretan says all Cretans are liars. If it is said by a Cretan and if it is true, then it would be a lie, and the statement would cancel itself out. It is not possible for a Cretan to say "all Cretans are liars" and assume that this statement applies absolutely. This shows you the pattern of absolutizing.

But every theory has to be applied to itself without crumbling. If you apply Freud's theory to Freud as he brings up unconscious soul content into consciousness, then you have to say that this theory is merely the outcome of the sexual life. Just as the statement that all Cretans are liars would be a lie if coming from a Cretan, so does the theory of the universality of the sexual drive crumble if you test it out by applying it to itself. And it is the same with other things. You may understand this principle for a long time without applying it vigorously in accordance with reality. It will be one of the special achievements of spiritual psychology that it can be applied to itself in this way.

LECTURE THREE
SUBCONSCIOUS AND SUPRACONSCIOUS
February 25, 1912

TODAY AND THE day after tomorrow I propose to discuss a few of the more important facts relating to consciousness and to karmic connections.

If you cast only a superficial glance at what exists in your soul from waking up in the morning to falling asleep at night — ideas, moods, impulses of will, adding of course all the impressions that approach the soul from the outside — then you have everything that may be called the contents of ordinary consciousness. It must be clear to us that all these details of our conscious activity are dependent, under ordinary conditions, on the instruments of the physical body. The immediate, irrefutable proof of this is that we must wake up in order to live within these facts of the ordinary consciousness. For us this means that we must descend into the physical body with what is outside the body during sleep, and the physical body must be at our disposal with its instruments if the activities of the ordinary consciousness are to take their course.

Now the following question arises: in what way do we as human beings, as soul and spiritual beings, make use of our physical instruments, our sense organs and nervous system, to live in our everyday consciousness? In the materialistic world out there, we find the belief that our physical instruments in fact produce what goes on in our consciousness. I have frequently pointed out that this is not the case; it is not true that we should think of our sense organs or the brain as producing the events in our consciousness in the same way that a candle brings forth a flame. The relationship between what we call consciousness and the bodily instruments is completely different. We can compare it with the relationship between a person looking into a mirror and the mirror. When we are sleeping, we live in our consciousness in the same way as if, let us say, we were walking straight ahead in a room. If we walk straight ahead in a room, we do not see ourselves, how our nose or forehead looks, and so forth. Only when someone comes toward us with a mirror do we behold ourselves. Then we are faced with what has existed all along, but now it also exists for us. It is the same with the contents of our ordinary consciousness. They exist continually within us, and as such they have nothing whatsoever to do with the physical body — as little as we ourselves have to do with the mirror mentioned above.

The materialistic theory concerning this is simply nonsense; it is not even a possible hypothesis. For what the materialists claim can only be compared with people saying that because they can see themselves in the mirror, the mirror has created them. If you want to delude yourself that the mirror creates you because you see yourself only when it is held up to you, then you can also believe that parts of the brain or of the sense organs produce the contents of your soul life. Both statements are equally "intelligent" and "true." That mirrors create human beings is just as true as that our brain produces thoughts. The contents of our consciousness persist. For our organization it is necessary that we be able to perceive these existing contents of consciousness. To this end we must face the reflection of our consciousness in our physical body. Thus our physical body is what we may call a reflecting apparatus for the contents of our ordinary consciousness. These contents exist in our soul and spiritual being, and we perceive them by holding up to them the mirror of our corporeality; we cannot perceive them directly in our soul, just as we cannot see ourselves without a mirror.

That is how things are. Of course our body is not just a passive reflecting apparatus, but there are all kinds of processes going on within it. So you can imagine that while a mirror is silvered on the surface to produce the reflection, beneath the surface of our physical body there are all sorts of processes going on. This comparison is sufficient to show the relationship between our spiritual and soul being and our body. What we want to keep in mind is that for everything we experience in our everyday consciousness our physical body is an adequate reflecting apparatus. Behind or, let us say, beneath the facts of ordinary consciousness lie the things that stream into our ordinary soul life and that we designate as contents living in the hidden depths of the soul.

Poets and artists experience something of what exists in the hidden depths of the soul, especially when they know, as genuine poets or artists, that they do not arrive at what they express in their works through ordinary thinking and logic or through sense perception. Instead these things emerge from the unknown depths where they exist without first having to be arranged by the forces of ordinary consciousness. But from these hidden depths of the soul other things also emerge, things that play a part in our everyday consciousness, although in everyday life we are unaware of their origin.

As we saw yesterday, we can go down deeper, into the realm of semiconsciousness, into the realm of dreams. And we know that dreams can bring up things from the hidden depths of soul life that we cannot lift up in the usual way just by exerting our consciousness. When an event long buried in memory appears before a person's soul in a dream picture, as happens again and again, the individual in most cases could never have lifted the event out of the hidden pits of soul life through recollection alone, because the ordinary consciousness does not extend so far down. But what is inaccessible to this ordinary consciousness is within easy reach for the unconscious. In the semiconscious state characteristic of dreams much that has been stored or preserved, so to speak, is brought up or allowed to rise up.

However, only those things come up that have not had the kind of effect usually produced by experiences that sink down into the hidden depths of the soul. We become healthy or ill, are in a bad mood or in a good mood, not because of the ordinary course of our life, but because a bodily condition results from the experiences that have sunk down. We can no longer remember them, but they are in the depths of our soul life and make us what we become in the course of life. Many people's lives would be quite comprehensible to us if we only knew what had descended into the depths throughout their lives. If we were able to trace their lives back into childhood, we would be able to understand many people in their thirties, forties, or fifties, and would know why they have this or that predisposition, why they feel so deeply dissatisfied in this or that area of life without themselves being able to pinpoint the causes. We would then be able to get an idea of how their parents and environment affected them, of the sorrow and joy, the pleasure and pain, that were evoked and still work on the total mood of the person even though the events themselves have probably been totally forgotten. For what streams out of our consciousness down into the hidden depths of the soul continues to work there.

It is a curious fact that what continues to work, works primarily upon ourselves and does not leave, so to speak, the sphere of our personality. Therefore when the clairvoyant consciousness descends — and this can happen through what we call imagination or imaginative cognition — when the clairvoyant consciousness descends to the realm of the unconscious where the things I have just described rule, then the person concerned always finds himself or herself.[1] The seeker finds what exists and surges within him or her. And that is good; for in true self-knowledge we must get to know ourselves by observing and familiarizing ourselves with all the driving forces at work within us.

If we penetrate with our clairvoyant consciousness into the unconscious by means of the exercises for imaginative cognition and do not notice that first of all we find only ourselves with all that lives and works in us, then we lay ourselves open to all kinds of errors. For nothing that can be compared to our ordinary contents of consciousness can make us aware that we are dealing only with ourselves. At one stage or another, we have the possibility, let us say, of having visions, seeing apparitions, that are new compared to what we know from experience. This may happen, but to believe that such things are part of the higher worlds would be a serious mistake. These things do not present themselves in the same way as things in our inner life appear to the ordinary consciousness. If we have a headache, that is a fact of our ordinary consciousness. We know that the pain is located in our head. If we have a stomach ache, we feel it within ourselves. If we descend into what we call the hidden depths of the soul, we remain absolutely within ourselves, and yet what we encounter may present itself as if it were outside of us.

Let us consider a striking example; let us assume that someone has a longing to be the reincarnation of Mary Magdalene. I have already told you that I have counted twenty-four such Mary Magdalenes in my lifetime! Let us assume also that the person does not yet admit this wish to himself or herself. After all, we do not need to admit our own wishes to our conscious mind; that is not necessary. So someone reads the story of Mary Magdalene in the Bible and likes it very much. The desire to be Mary Magdalene can arise at once in the unconscious mind while in the ordinary or surface consciousness there is nothing but a liking for this character. Unbeknownst to the person, there lives a growing desire to be Mary Magdalene in the unconscious. This individual goes through the world, and as long as nothing intervenes, there is this liking for Mary Magdalene in the ordinary consciousness, that is to say, as far as this person knows, he or she simply likes Mary Magdalene. The ardent desire to *be* Mary Magdalene lives in the unconscious, but the person knows nothing of that and so is not troubled by it. The person's life is guided by the contents of the ordinary consciousness, and this fierce desire may never enter his or her conscious mind.

But let us assume that as a result of applying some esoteric practice or other, this person can reach his or her unconscious and enter into it. The desire to be Mary Magdalene may not be perceived the way we become aware of a headache. In fact if it were perceived this way, then the person could be reasonable and sensible, and react to this desire as he or she would react to a headache, namely, by trying to get rid of it. But because of the person's irregular penetration into the unconscious, that is not what happens. Instead the desire presents itself as a fact outside the person and appears as the vision: you are Mary Magdalene! It stands before the individual, projecting itself as a fact. And at the current stage of evolution, human beings are not able to control such things with their I. With good, correct, and careful schooling this cannot happen, for then the I goes along into every sphere; but as soon as something happens without the I going along, such visions appear as objective facts. The observer in question believes himself or herself to be recalling the events surrounding Mary Magdalene, and identifies with her. This is a real possibility.

I emphasize this possibility today so you may see that only careful schooling and caution regarding our entrance into the domain of occultism can save us from falling into error. We must keep in mind that we must first see a whole world before us and must perceive objects and events around us, but not things we relate to ourselves or that are within us even though they appear as a world tableau. We will do well at first to consider what we see only as a projection of our own inner life; then we are well protected from errors along this way. This is the best of all: as a general rule, regard *everything* as phenomena emanating from yourself. Most of them arise out of our wishes, vanities, and aspirations, in short, out of characteristics connected with our egoism.

For the most part these things project themselves outward, and you may now ask: How can we avoid these errors? How can we save ourselves from them? We cannot save ourselves from these errors through the ordinary contents of consciousness. The error comes about when we cannot escape from ourselves and are all entangled in ourselves although, in reality, we are facing a world tableau. From this you can see that it is crucial that in some way we get out of ourselves and learn somehow to distinguish: here is one vision and there another. The visions are both outside ourselves; one is perhaps only the projection of a desire, while the other is a fact. However, the difference between them is not as great as that between the headache someone else has and the one you have. Our own inner life is projected out into space and so is the inner life of other persons. How can we distinguish between them?

We must learn to distinguish true from false impressions within the occult domain even though they are mixed up and all appear with the same claim to authenticity. It is as though we looked into the physical world and saw imaginary trees in addition to real ones; we would not be able to tell the difference between them. If both real and imaginary trees were there, we would see real, objective facts, which are independent of us, as well as those arising only from our own inner life. How can we learn to distinguish between these two intermingled realms?

We do not learn this primarily through our consciousness. If we remain entirely within the confines of our mental life, there is no possibility of differentiation. This possibility lies only in the slow occult training of the soul. As we advance further and further, we learn to distinguish, that is, to do in the sphere of the occult what we would have to do if we saw real and imaginary trees next to each other on the physical plane. We can walk through the imaginary trees, but we meet real resistance if we try to do that with real trees. Something similar must confront us in the realm of the occult, although of course only as a spiritual fact.

If we go about it in the right way, we can learn in a fairly simple way to distinguish between the true and false in this realm, not through ideas, but through a decision of our will. This resolution may be brought about in the following way: If we look back at our life, we find two clearly different groups of events. We often find that this or that success or failure is related to our abilities. We can understand that we do not succeed very well in a certain field because we are not particularly bright in this area. On the other hand, in areas where we assume we have some ability, we find our success quite natural.

Perhaps we need not always see so clearly the connection between what we do and our abilities. There is also a less definite way to realize this connection. For example, if someone in the later years of life is pursued by this or that misfortune, then that person can think back and say, "I did little to make myself strong and energetic," or "I was always careless and irresponsible." On the other hand, the person may also say, "I do not fully understand the connection between my lack of success and the things I did, but I do see that things cannot always turn out as well for a careless, lazy person as they do for a conscientious and industrious one." In short, we can understand some of our successes and failures, but for others we cannot discover their connection to our abilities. Then we feel that although we have this or that ability and therefore should have been successful in this or that undertaking, it nevertheless did not succeed. Thus there is clearly a type of success or failure whose connection with our abilities we cannot see right away.

There are also certain things that meet us as blows of fate in the outside world, and regarding these we can sometimes say that they do after all appear fair and just, for we have actually furnished all the preconditions for these things. However, other things happen that we cannot explain. Thus there are two types of experiences: those due to us, whose connection to our abilities we realize, and those that are inexplicable. Our external experiences fall likewise into two classes: those of which we cannot say we have produced their preconditions, and others where we know we have brought about the conditions that allowed them to happen.

Now let us look around a little at our lives. Here is a useful experiment for everyone. We could gather together all the things we cannot see the causes of, that is, successes that led us to say, "Even a fool can be right sometimes" — in short, successes we cannot attribute to ourselves. We can do the same for failures and for those seemingly accidental outer events for which we know of no motivating influence. And now we can make the following experiment: We construct in our mind an artificial human being, so to speak, who through his own abilities brought about all those of our successes we cannot explain. If we succeeded in something that required wisdom in an area where we are stupid, then we imagine a person who is particularly clever in this field, and who simply had to succeed. Or in the case of an outer event, we proceed in this way: let us say a brick falls on our head. We can see no reason for this, but we imagine someone who brought it about by running up to the roof and loosening the brick, so that it could only be a short time before it must fall down. Then this person runs down quickly, and the brick hits him. We can do this with events that with our ordinary consciousness we know we have not brought about, events that sometimes happen very much against our will.

Let us assume that at some time in our life someone has hit us. To make this less difficult, let us place this event back in our childhood. Let us imagine we had somehow employed somebody to spank us, that we had indeed done everything possible to get this spanking. In short, we imagine a human being who takes upon himself everything we cannot account for. If we want to progress in occultism, we must do many things that run contrary to the ordinary course of events. If you do only what generally seems reasonable, you will not get far in occultism, for things relating to higher worlds may at first seem quite foolish. It does not matter that our method here seems foolish to the prosaic people in the outer world.

At any rate, we construct this human being in our mind. At first it seems to us merely grotesque to do this, perhaps even without understanding the reason for it. However, everyone who tries this will make a strange discovery, namely, the astonishing discovery that he or she no longer wants to get rid of this being but rather begins to find it interesting. If you try it, you will see for yourself: you cannot get away from this artificial human being; it lives within you. And strangely enough, it not only lives within us, but it also transforms itself radically to such an extent that at last it becomes something completely different from what it had been. It turns into something we must admit indeed exists within us.

This is an experience everyone can have. We can realize that what I have just described — not the original human being we created in our fantasy, but what has become of it — is part of what is within us. Now this is just what has, so to speak, brought about the things in our life that have apparently no causes. Thus we find within ourselves the real cause of what otherwise cannot be explained. In other words, what I have described to you is not only the way to look into your own soul life and find something, but also the way from the soul life into the environment. For our failures do not remain with us, but belong to our environment. We have taken something out of our environment that does not agree with the facts of our consciousness, but presents itself as if it were within us. Then we get the feeling that we really have something to do with events that seem to have no cause in real life. In this way we get a sense of our connection with our destiny, with what is called *karma*. This soul experiment opens for us a way to experience karma within ourselves.

You may say that you do not fully understand what I have said. But if you say that, it is not because you do not understand what you think you cannot understand; rather you do not comprehend something even a child can grasp, simply because you have not thought of it. It is impossible for anyone who has not carried out the experiment to understand these things. Only those who have done this experiment can understand. What I have said is nothing else than the description of an experiment everyone can do and experience. Everyone can come to the realization that something lives within us that is connected with our karma. If people knew this from the outset, we would not need to give them a method for attaining this knowledge.

It is quite all right that people who have not made the experiment do not comprehend what I said. However, it is not a question of understanding information about something our soul can do. When our soul follows such paths, it becomes used not only to living within itself, in its own wishes and desires, but to seeing its relationship to outer events and to considering them. That is what our soul gets used to through this experiment. It is precisely the things we have not wished for that we have built into what we have spoken about. Then we can face our destiny in such a way that we can calmly take it upon us. And when we can say about those things we usually grumble and rebel against, "We accept them willingly, for we have imposed them on ourselves," a state of mind and heart develops that allows us to distinguish with absolute certainty between what is true and false on our way down into the hidden depths of the soul. Then it will be wonderfully clear and obvious what is true and what is false.

If you see a vision with your inner eye and can drive it away, banish it, as it were, by a mere look — simply through using all the forces you feel within you and have come to know — then it is just a phantom. But if you cannot get rid of it in this way, if you can banish at most what reminds you of the outer world while the really visionary part, the spiritual, still remains like a solid fact — then it is a true vision. But you cannot make this distinction until you have done what I have described. Without the above-mentioned schooling, there can be no certainty in distinguishing between the true and false on the supersensible plane. The essential thing in this soul experiment is that we always remain in full possession of our ordinary consciousness in everything we desire. Through this experiment we get used to considering what we do not at all want in our ordinary consciousness, what is repugnant to us, as something we have willed into existence. We may have advanced to a certain degree of inner development, but we will make one mistake after another unless through such an experiment we counterbalance the wishes, desires, sympathies, and antipathies in our soul with our connection to what we did not want.

The greatest mistake in the Theosophical Society was made by Helena Petrovna Blavatsky when she fixed her spiritual attention upon the realm where Christ may be found while in her wishes and desires — in short, in her ordinary consciousness — she had a lasting antipathy, even a passionate loathing, for everything Christian or Hebrew and a preference for all other spiritual cultures on earth.[2] And because she had never gone through what has been described today, her notion of the Christ naturally was completely wrong. She passed it on to her closest students, and since then it has been dragged along, over-simplified to the point of grotesqueness, into the present day. These things extend to the highest spheres. Seeing many things on the occult plane is different from being able to distinguish between them. This must be strongly emphasized.

When we immerse ourselves into our hidden soul depths — and every clairvoyant must do this — we first come into what is fundamentally ourselves. And we must get to know our-selves by really making the transition that begins with looking at a world whose kingdoms Lucifer and Ahriman always promise to give us. This means our own inner self is put before us, and the devil says it is the objective world. That is the temp-tation even Christ did not escape. The illusions of his own inner world were presented, but through his inherent power, he recognized from the very beginning that this is not a real world, but a world that is within. It is from this inner world alone, which we must separate into two parts — one of which, namely our own personal part, we can get rid of while the other remains — that we pass through the hidden depths of our soul life out into the objective supersensible world.

Just as our spiritual-soul core must make use of our physi-cal body as a mirror to perceive the outer world and the con-tents of ordinary consciousness, so it must make use of our etheric body as a reflecting apparatus to perceive the super-sensible facts confronting us. The higher sense organs, if we may call them that, appear within the astral body, but what lives in them must be reflected by the etheric body, just as the spiritual and soul activity we are aware of in our everyday life is reflected by the physical body. We must now learn to manage our etheric body. We are usually not aware of our etheric body, although it vitalizes us. Naturally we must first get to know it before we can become able to recognize what enters into us from the supersensible world outside us and is reflected by our etheric body.

What we experience when we descend into the hidden depths of our soul life and experience first of all ourselves — that is, the projection of our wishes — resembles the life in *kamaloka*.[3] The only difference is that when we advance in our ordinary life to this state of being imprisoned in ourselves — for that is what we must call it — we can still return to our physical body, but in *kamaloka* the physical body is gone and so is that part of the etheric body that primarily reflects us. Instead, the universal life-ether surrounding us serves as an instrument of reflection and mirrors everything within us. Thus, when we are in *kamaloka*, our own inner world, all our wishes and desires, our feelings and moods, is built up as an objective world around us.

It is important to understand that the primary characteristic of our life in *kamaloka* is our imprisonment within ourselves, and this prison is the more securely bolted because we cannot return to the physical life our whole inner activity was geared to. Only when we live through our *kamaloka* period in such a way that we gradually realize — and the realization does come only gradually — that we can get rid of everything around us if we experience ourselves other than through mere desires and so forth, only then does our *kamaloka* prison burst open.

What does this mean? Let us suppose that someone dies

with a certain wish; this wish is part of what projects itself outward and is built up around him in some kind of form.

As long as this wish lives within this person, he cannot open *kamaloka* with any key in regard to it. But when he realizes that this wish can be satisfied only when it is discarded, when it is given up and is no longer wished — that is, when it is torn out of his soul and his attitude toward it becomes the opposite of what it had been — then gradually everything that imprisons him in *kamaloka* will be torn from the soul together with the wish. Only then do we come into the realm between death and a new birth that has been called the *devachanic* realm, which we can also enter through clairvoyance when we have recognized what belongs only to our self.[4] In clairvoyance we reach this point at a certain stage of maturity in our development; in *kamaloka* it comes simply as a result of the passage of time, simply because time so torments us through our own desires that at last they are overcome. Then what we were led to believe was the world and its splendor is destroyed.

The world of supersensible realities is usually called *devachan*. How does this world of supersensible facts meet us? Here, on our earth, we can speak of *devachan* only because in clairvoyance, when the self has really been overcome, we enter the world of supersensible facts, which objectively exist and coincide with what is present in *devachan*.

The most important characteristic of the *devachanic* world is that moral and physical facts and laws can no longer be distinguished. Moral and physical laws have become one and the same. What does that mean? Well, is it not true that in the physical world the sun shines upon the just and the unjust? Those who commit a crime may be put in prison, but the physical sun is not darkened. That is to say, in the physical world there is a realm of moral laws and a realm of physical laws, and both go their separate ways.

It is not so in *devachan*, not at all. There everything proceeding from morality, from intelligent wisdom, from the aesthetically beautiful, and so on, leads to creation, while everything that arises from immorality, intellectual untruths, and ugliness leads to deterioration and destruction. There the laws of nature are such that the sun does not shine upon the just and the unjust alike, but, if we may speak figuratively, it darkens before the unjust. The just people passing through *devachan* have spiritual sunshine, that is, the influence of the fructifying forces that help them in life. These spiritual forces draw back from the dishonest or nasty person. There things are possible that are impossible here on earth.

Here, when two people, one who is just and one unjust, walk side by side, the sun cannot shine on one without also shining on the other. However, in the spiritual world the effect of the spiritual forces on people depends absolutely on the quality of the individual concerned. The laws of nature and of the spirit do not go their separate ways, but follow one and the same path. That is the fundamental truth. In the *devachanic* world the natural laws and the moral and intellectual ones work together as one.

As a result when we enter the *devachanic* world and live there, we have within us all the justice and injustice, good and evil, beauty and ugliness, truth and falsehood from our last life. All this acts there in such a way that it takes immediate possession of the natural laws. For example, in terms of the physical world, we would describe the law there as follows: If someone in the physical world had stolen or lied and then went out into the sun, that person would find that the sun no longer shone on him, and gradually this lack of sunshine would make him ill. Or let us imagine that someone in the physical world told a lie and then had difficulty breathing. That is an analogy to what would be the case in the *devachanic* world. To the person who had burdened his conscience with this or that, something happens in his spiritual and soul nature so that the natural law, at the same time and absolutely, expresses the spiritual law. As this person continues to live and develop further through the *devachanic* world, gradually more and more properties will permeate him that will make him an expression of the qualities he brought with him from the previous life.

Let us suppose that someone lives in *devachan* for 200 years after having lied much in a previous life. This person indeed lives in *devachan*, but the spirits of truth withdraw from him. There dies in him what in a truthful soul would come to life. Or let us assume that someone with a pronounced trait of vanity, which he has not given up, goes through *devachan*. In *devachan* this vanity is an extraordinarily evil-smelling emanation, and certain spiritual beings avoid a personality who gives out the offensive smell of ambition or vanity. This is not a figurative statement. In *devachan* vanity and ambition are extremely malodorous and lead certain beings to withdraw, so their beneficent influence is lost. This is like expecting a plant to grow in the cellar although it requires sunlight to thrive. A vain person cannot thrive. He will grow up under the influence of this characteristic. When he reincarnates, he lacks the strength to incorporate good influences. Instead of developing certain organs in a healthy way, he forms an unhealthy organ system in his body.

Thus what we will become can be seen not only from our

physical conditions but also from our moral and intellectual ones. Only when we emerge from the spiritual plane do natural and spiritual laws go their separate, parallel ways. Between death and a new birth they form a unity. And the natural forces implanted in our soul are destructive if they are the result of immoral deeds in past lives, but fruitful if they are the result of noble actions. This is true not only for our inner constitution, but also for what meets us from outside as our karma.

In *devachan* the essential fact is that no difference exists between natural and spiritual laws, and it is the same for the clairvoyant who really penetrates to the supersensible worlds. The supersensible worlds are radically different from what we have on the physical plane. It is simply impossible for the clairvoyant to take the materialistic view that something is *only* an objective law of nature. Behind this objective natural law a spiritual law always stands. A clairvoyant cannot cross a parched meadow or a flooded district, cannot see the eruption of a volcano without thinking that behind the facts of nature there are spiritual forces, spiritual beings. For the clairvoyant, the eruption of a volcano is at the same time also a moral deed, even though its morality may lie in an entirely different, undreamed-of realm.

People who always confuse the physical with the higher worlds will say, "When innocent human beings are destroyed in the eruption of a volcano, one cannot assume that it is a moral deed." Such a judgment would be as cruelly philistine as the opposite one, namely, to regard the eruption as a punishment from God for the people living near the volcano. Both judgments are possible only from the narrow-minded standpoint of the physical world. Much more universal things may be at stake here. Those who live on the slope of a volcano and whose property is destroyed when it erupts may in fact be entirely innocent as far as this life is concerned. It will be made up to them later. This does not mean that we should be hardhearted and not help them; that would again be a narrow-minded interpretation of the facts. Nevertheless it is true that in the case of volcanic eruptions there is the fact that human beings do certain things in the course of earth evolution that retard human evolution. And the good gods must work to compensate for that, and so such natural phenomena sometimes are necessary to create a counterbalance.

The connections between such things can sometimes be seen only in occult depths. In this way things human beings have done counter to the true spiritual course of their development can find compensation. Every event, even if it seems to be a mere phenomenon of nature, is at bottom a moral matter. And spiritual beings in the higher worlds are the bearers of the moral law behind the physical facts. If you imagine a world where there is no separation of natural and spiritual laws, in other words, a world where justice rules as a natural law, then you have the *devachanic* world. In this *devachanic* world crimes are not punished through some kind of arbitrary measures; rather that which is immoral destroys itself as inexorably as fire consumes combustible substances. By the same token morality advances on its own.

We thus see that the essential characteristic, the innermost heart, so to speak, of existence is quite different in the different worlds. We cannot get an idea of these different worlds if we do not consider these radically different peculiarities. We can now correctly characterize the physical world, *kamaloka*, and *devachan* as follows. In the physical world, natural and spiritual laws run side by side as two series of facts. In *kamaloka*, human beings are confined within themselves, as if in the prison of their own being. The *devachanic* world is the complete opposite of the physical; there natural and spiritual law are one and the same. These are the three characteristics. If you consider them carefully and try to get a feeling for how very different from our own a world must be where moral and intellectual laws, and even the law of beauty are at the same time natural laws, you will get a sense of what the *devachanic* world is like.

When we meet an ugly person in our physical world, we have no right to treat him as if he were to be rejected in soul-spiritual terms. Nor do we have the right to treat a beautiful person as if he were necessarily in soul-spiritual terms worthy of high esteem. In *devachan* it is quite different. There we meet no ugliness that is not deserved. At the same time a person who has an ugly face in this incarnation because of his deeds in the previous one and who strove throughout this life to be true and honest will surely not meet us in *devachan* in an ugly form. Rather he will certainly have transformed his ugliness into beauty. But it is equally true that people who are dishonest, vain, or ambitious in this life will wander about in *devachan* in an ugly shape. Moreover in ordinary physical life, we do not see that an ugly face continually robs itself of something while a beautiful face gives something to itself. However, in *devachan* ugliness is an element of continuous destruction, while we will not see anything beautiful without assuming that it is the result of an equally continuous furtherance and stimulation.

Thus we must feel quite differently toward the *devachanic* or mental world than toward the physical world. And it is necessary to differentiate between these sensations and to see what is essential and crucial so that you learn not only the outer description of these things, but also absorb feelings and impressions toward the things spiritual psychology describes. if you try to advance to an appreciation of a world where morality, beauty, and intellectual truth appear as inexorable as natural law, then you have a sense of the *devachanic* world. This is why we must, so to speak, collect so much material and work so much, so that we can ultimately forge what we have gained into one feeling.

It is impossible for anyone to come easily to a real knowledge of what must gradually be presented to the world through spiritual science. There are many different movements that say, "Why must we learn so many things in spiritual psychology? Are we to become pupils again? After all, *feeling* is all that matters." It does indeed matter, but it must be the right feeling, which must first be developed. This is true of everything. It would be nice, would it not, for the painter if he did not have to learn the technique of his art, if he did not have to paint the picture slowly on the canvas, if he needed only to blow on his hands to have his finished work before him? It is strange that in our world the more people approach the realm of the soul, the harder it is for them to realize that merely blowing on one's hands is not enough. Nobody will accept that anyone can be a composer without first learning about music; there it is quite obvious. People are almost, though not quite, as willing to admit that the same is true for painting. For poetry they admit it even less, otherwise there would be fewer poets in our time. For actually no time is as unpoetic as our own, although there are so many poets. People think it is not necessary to have studied poetry; one only needs to be able to write, which naturally has nothing to do with poetry — and, of course, to spell correctly — and to express one's thoughts properly. And for philosophy still less seems required.

Today it is taken for granted that anyone can easily judge anything concerning worldviews and philosophies of life, since everyone has his or her own standpoint. We find again and again that it does not count for much when someone has painstakingly used various means and methods of inner work to research and to know something in the world. Instead it is accepted as a matter of course that the standpoint of those who have labored long before venturing to say a little about the secrets of the world is given the same value as that of people who simply have decided that they too will have a standpoint. These days everyone has a worldview.

And being a Theosophist, according to some, is still easier; it does not require more than accepting, in one's own individual fashion, only the first of the three basic principles of the Theosophical Society, rather than all of them. This first principle really asks nothing more than that one should with more or less sincerity admit to be a loving person — it doesn't matter whether one really is loving or not — and so one is simply a Theosophist and then has the right feeling. Thus, when we consider the requirements for passing judgments and evaluating standpoints, we see a continuous decline from music through matters that require less and less until we end with Theosophy. There it is enough — and this would not suffice in painting — that one just blows on one's hands. We form the core of the brotherhood of all human beings; that makes us Theosophists! We do not need to learn anything.

However, what really matters is that we work with all our energy so that we can finally gather what we have thus acquired and carry it over into feelings which will color it and thus make it the highest, truest knowledge. Struggle through and work your way to such a feeling that belongs to the impression of a world where natural and spiritual law coincide. Then if you work seriously — no matter how much you exerted yourself in working through this or that theory — it will make an impression on the *devachanic* world. If you have not simply imagined a feeling, but developed it through years of careful work, then this feeling, these nuances of sensitivity, have a strength that will carry you further than they could reach of themselves; for then they have become true through serious and conscientious study. Then you are not far from the point where these nuances burst open, and there lies before you the reality of *devachan*. For if the nuances of feeling are truly acquired through work, they become a capacity for perception.

Therefore, if we really and truly work in our branch groups, not for sensations, but based on honesty and patient practice, then our meeting places will become what they should be: schools to lead people into the realms of clairvoyance. And only those who cannot wait for this, or who do not want to join us in working, can maintain a wrong view of these matters.

LECTURE FOUR
HIDDEN DEPTHS OF THE SOUL
February 27, 1912

W E HAVE RECENTLY begun talking about the existence of hidden soul depths, and it will be good to continue to occupy ourselves with various details of this subject that may be useful for students of spiritual psychology. Generally speaking, it must be said that a complete explanation and understanding of these things can be worked out only on the basis of what spiritual psychology gives us.

We have considered the human organization from various viewpoints. Therefore you will easily be able to connect in the right way what appears when we look into the hidden depths of the soul with the human organization as we know it from the more or less elementary presentations based on the worldview of spiritual psychology.

It has been repeatedly said that everything in our mental images and perceptions, our impulses of will, our feelings — in short, all that goes on in our souls in the normal condition between waking up and falling asleep — may be called the activities, characteristics, and powers of our ordinary consciousness. Now we will represent in a diagram everything that is part of this ordinary consciousness, everything we know and feel and will between waking up and falling asleep, by enclosing it between these two parallel lines (see drawing, line a–b).

In this section (a–b) belongs our imagination as well as every kind of perception. When we establish contact with the outer world and are in touch with it through our senses, and thus get a picture of this world through all kinds of connected sensory impressions, this is also part of our ordinary consciousness. All our feelings and impulses of will belong to it as well — in short, everything contained in our ordinary consciousness. One could say that everything our normal soul activities tell us about in our everyday life belongs in the area defined by these parallel lines (a–b).

The point is for us to know with certainty that this so-called soul life depends on using the physical body as its instrument, including the senses and the nervous system. If we contrast these parallel lines with two others, we can say that our sense organs and nervous system are the tools or instruments for this consciousness, and the sense organs probably to a greater extent than the nervous system.

Beneath the threshold of this ordinary consciousness lies

creative, physical world	sense organs, nervous system	mental images, perceptions, feelings, impulses of will	a
elemental world	heat forces of the blood, breathing forces	hidden aspects of the soul life, unconscious, imagination, inspiration, intuition, premonitions, second sight[1]	b c

everything we can enclose between other parallel lines and can describe as the hidden sides of our soul life or as the unconscious (see diagram, b–c). We get a good idea of what is embedded in this subconscious layer if we remember that through spiritual training human beings can develop imagination, inspiration, and intuition. Just as we must place mental images, feelings, and impulses of will in the ordinary consciousness, so we have to locate imagination, inspiration, and intuition in the subconscious. As we know, the subconscious becomes active not only as a result of spiritual training, but also as the legacy of a primeval, primitive state of conscious-ness, that is, as an atavism. In that case, there appear what we call visions, and these visions of this naïve, primitive con-sciousness correspond to the imaginations achieved through training. Premonitions appear also, and they are the primitive equivalent of inspiration. We will immediately see from a sig-nificant example what the difference is between an inspira-tion and a premonition.

We have already mentioned that in the course of the twen-tieth century there will occur in human evolution what may be called a sort of spiritual return of Christ. There will be a number of persons who will experience in an etheric form this working of Christ from the astral plane into our world. We can find out about this fact by learning what the course of evolution is through careful training and by realizing as a result of this schooling that this event must happen in the twentieth century as described. However, it can also happen, as it often does at the present time, that here and there indi-viduals are gifted with a natural, primitive clairvoyance and then have a kind of obscure inspiration, which we may call a premonition, of the approach of Christ. Perhaps such people do not know exactly what is involved; yet even so important an inspiration as this can indeed appear in the form of a pre-monition if something occurs in the primitive consciousness that is more than a mere premonition or vision. The vision consists in putting some sort of picture in the place of a spir-itual process.

Let us say, for example, that someone has lost a friend whose I has passed through the gate of death. This friend now dwells in the spiritual world, and a kind of bond establishes itself between the deceased and the one still living in this world. It is possible that the latter cannot rightly understand what the deceased wants from him and has a false idea of what his dead friend experiences. The connection between them presents itself in a vision that, as a picture, may be false though founded upon the fact that the dead one is indeed trying to establish a bond with the living person. This manifests itself as a premonition, so that the living person knows certain things, either concerning the past or the future, that are inaccessible to normal consciousness. When the human soul has a clear perception (not just a vision, which may possibly be false, but a distinct perception) of an occurrence, let us say, in the sense world, but in this case in a sphere invisible to the physical senses, or of an incident in the supersensible world — this is called *deuteroscopy* or second sight in occultism. With all this I have described to you only what takes place in the human soul, and only in the subconscious, whether it has been achieved through proper training or it appears as natural clairvoyance.

As to the difference between the unconscious and our ordinary consciousness, what goes on here in the human soul itself is very different from the processes in the ordinary consciousness. The relationship between the processes of our ordinary consciousness and everything they are concerned with is such that people have spoken of the impotence of ordinary consciousness. The eyes see a rose, but regardless of our perceptions and ideas about roses, the eyes, which are so constituted that the image of the rose arises in our consciousness, have no power over the blooming, growth, and withering of the rose. The rose grows and withers because of the forces of nature, but our eyes cannot perceive anything but the immediate present as long as only our ordinary consciousness is at work.

This is not true of the facts and events in our subconscious. And this is what we must keep in mind, for it is extremely important. When we perceive something with our eyes in the normal process of seeing, for example, colors or anything else, we cannot alter the objective facts in any way by mere perception. In fact if nothing else happens to our eyes, they also remain unchanged by the mere act of seeing. It is only when we go beyond normal light to blinding light that we injure our eyes. Thus we can say that if we limit ourselves to the contents of normal consciousness, we do not even have any effect on ourselves. Our organism is so constituted that the processes of ordinary consciousness usually do not cause changes in us.

It is quite different with what appears in the unconscious. let us assume that we are forming an image or having a vision of a good being. This good being is not in the physical but in the supersensible world. Now let us place the world of these beings that we perceive in an act of the imagination or vision between these lines (see p. 103, b–c). In that world we have to seek all the perceptions and objects of our unconscious.

Now when we picture an evil or demonic being from this world in an act of the imagination or vision, then we are not as powerless in regard to this being as our eyes are over the rose. When we have an image or vision of an evil being and develop for this completely clear, visionary image a feeling that the being should depart, the latter must of necessity feel itself powerfully pushed or thrust away from us. The same principle applies when we have an image or vision of a good being. If we develop a sympathetic feeling, the good being feels impelled to approach us and connect itself with us. All beings of this world feel our attracting or repelling forces when we form visions of them.

Thus our eyes would be in the same position as our subconscious if they would not only see a rose, but could also through seeing it develop the desire that the rose approach and actually draw it to them — or as if your eyes on seeing something disgusting would not only conclude that it is disgusting, but would also be able to make the disgusting thing go away merely through their antipathy. The subconscious is in touch with a world where the sympathy and antipathy in the human soul have an effect. It is necessary to bring this before our souls.

Sympathy and antipathy and all other subconscious impulses affect this world in the way described as well as everything within us, everything that is part of our etheric body. They even affect certain forces of the physical body, all of which we have to picture as enclosed by these parallel lines. We have to picture enclosed here everything that lives in us as the forces that pulsate through our blood — its heat force, as well as another force that lies in our healthy or unhealthy breathing, which is more or less determined by our whole organism — in other words, the condition of our breathing forces. (See diagram, b–c.) In addition, our subconscious also works on a large part of our etheric body. The subconscious or hidden soul powers work within us and affect the heat forces of our blood. These in turn determine our pulse rate, the vitality or sluggishness of our blood circulation, so our subconscious is necessarily connected with our blood circulation. Whether somebody has a quicker or more sluggish circulation depends essentially on the forces of the person's subconscious.

The demonic or good beings in the world out there can only be influenced when we have visions or images or other perceptions of a certain clarity in our subconscious, that is, when we see them standing before us. It is only then that sympathy or antipathy evoke certain forces as though by magic, and these forces then become active in that world. However, in terms of the influence on our own inner organism, consisting of what we have written down here (see diagram, p.103), it is not necessary that we have such clear pictures before our soul in our subconscious. Whether we know which imaginations correspond to a particular sympathy or not, the sympathy will affect our blood circulation, our breathing system, and our etheric body.

Let us assume a person has prevailing sensations of nausea for a certain time. If this person were a visionary or had imaginative sight, he or she would see these visions and images that are really perceptions of his or her own being, as I described the day before yesterday. They would be projected into space, but would nevertheless belong to the person's own inner world. These visions and imaginations would represent the force of the nausea living in him or her. Ye, even if the person could not practice this kind of self-knowledge and simply had nausea, it would live and work on him or her. The sensations of nausea would influence the heat forces of the blood and the person's forces of breathing. Thus it is indeed true that we have more or less healthy breathing and a more or less healthy blood circulation depending on whether we experience this or that in our subconscious. The activity of the etheric body with all its processes is especially dependent on the world of feelings living in us.

However, as becomes clear when the contents of the unconscious mind are really experienced by the soul, not only is there such a connection, but its existence exerts a continuous influence on the general condition of the human being. In other words, certain feelings and emotions enter into the unconscious, where they cause certain conditions of the heat forces of the blood, of the breathing power, and of the etheric body, and thus are beneficial to the organism or inhibit the individual's whole life. As a result of what enters into the subconscious, then, something in the person is always in the process of coming into being or dying away. Through what we send from our conscious mind down into the subconscious we are either depriving ourselves of our life forces or adding to them.

For example, if we take pleasure in a lie we have told, if we are not horrified at it, which would be the normal feeling about lies, but instead are indulgent or even feel satisfaction, then the feelings we have added to the lie are sent down into the subconscious. These impair the circulation, breathing, and the forces of the etheric body. As a result, in regard to everything we retain after going through the portal of death, we will have become stunted and will have deprived ourselves of energies. Something will have died in us that would have lived if we had felt the normal loathing and disgust for the lie. Then these feelings of loathing at the lie would have descended and would have affected the forces we have indicated here (see diagram, p.103), and we would have sent something beneficial, namely, creative forces, into our organism.

We see that we are indeed working on our coming into being and dying away out of our subconscious because it continuously receives forces from our upper or ordinary consciousness. In their present condition human beings are not yet powerful enough to corrupt other parts of their organism besides the blood circulation, the breathing, and the etheric body through their soul activity. They cannot impair the coarser and more solid parts of the physical organism; they can corrupt, so to speak, only a part of their organism. We can see especially clearly what has been impaired when what remains of the etheric body — which is in constant interaction with the heat forces of the blood and the condition of our breathing — has been influenced in this way: then it atrophies because of bad feelings. By the same token, it receives stimulating, strengthening, and beneficial forces through good, normal, and sincere feelings. We can say, therefore, that through the processes in their subconscious, human beings work directly on the growth and dying away, that is, on the real processes, the reality, of their organism. They descend from the region of powerlessness in the ordinary consciousness to a region where something comes into being and dies away in their own soul, and consequently in their entire organism.

We have seen that because the subconscious can more or less be experienced by the soul, something may be known about it and it also exerts an influence on a world sphere we can designate (with an expression used throughout the Middle Ages) the elemental world. We cannot enter directly into a relationship with this elemental world; we can do so only indirectly by having those experiences within us that result from the influence of the subconscious on the organism. After some time, when we have come to know ourselves so well that we can say: if we feel this and send down this or that feeling resulting from our conduct into our subconscious, we destroy certain things or cripple them, but if we have other experiences and send down different feelings, we do something beneficial for ourselves. In short, when we experience this ebb and flow of destructive and beneficent forces in us for a time, we will become more and more mature in our self-knowledge. That is what true self-knowledge really is.

This can be explained only by an analogy. The self-knowledge we gain in this way is as though a scorpion were biting off one of our toes every time we lie or do not have the proper feelings about a lie arising within us. No doubt if people felt such a real effect of their lies, they would not lie as much as they now do. A crippling of our organism in the physical world can be compared with what really happens, though we usually do not perceive it, through those daily experiences we send down into the subconscious mind. What is sent down because of our tolerant attitude toward a lie is such that it does bite off something and take it away from us, and the loss stunts us. In our future karma we must then regain what we lost. If we send down a right feeling into the subconscious mind — there is naturally an almost endless scale of feelings that may descend — we grow and create new life forces in our organism. Observing our own coming into being and dying away is the first stage of true self-knowledge.

People have told me that in the last lecture they did not fully understand how to distinguish between a genuine vision or image belonging to the realm of the objective and something that appears out there in space but really belongs to our own subjective nature.[2] I cannot tell you to write down this or that rule so that then you will be able to make the distinction. There are no such rules. One learns this gradually in the course of development. And we will be able to correctly distinguish between what belongs to us and what is an outer vision and belongs to a real being only after we have first endured the experience of having deadly subconscious processes continuously eating away at us. Then are equipped with a kind of certainty.

Then we also reach the state where we can confront a vision or image and know that we can penetrate it with the power of our spiritual sight. If the vision persists when this active force of seeing is turned upon it, then it is an objective fact. If the active force of our spiritual sight extinguishes the vision, it was obviously only our own creation. People who are not careful to do this may be looking at thousands and thousands of pictures from the akashic record, but if they do not test them to see whether or not they will be extinguished by a resolutely active gaze, they will see the akashic pictures, which can tell us so much, only as images of their own inner life. It could happen — it is not likely, but it could happen — that somebody sees nothing but his or her own inner life, projected into dramatic pictures and extended throughout the entire Atlantean world, throughout generations of human evolution. In spite of their apparent objectivity, these pictures may be nothing else but the projection of the individual's own inner self.

When we have passed through the portal of death, the obstructions no longer exist through which something subjective within us becomes an objective vision or image. In our everyday life nowadays, what we experience in our subconscious, what we send into our subconscious, does not always become a vision or image. It becomes an image through proper training, a vision in the case of atavistic clairvoyance. As soon as we have passed through the gate of death, all our inner life becomes at once an objective world; it is simply there. Essentially, *kamaloka* is nothing else but a world built up around us out of what we experience in our own soul. This condition is reversed only in *devachan*.

Thus we can easily understand what I have said about the effect of the sympathy or antipathy in visions, Imaginations, Inspirations, premonitions, and so on. In any case, they influence the objective elemental world. I said about this effect that as long as human beings are incarnated physically, only what they have developed into vision or imagination affects this elemental world. In the case of the dead, however, the forces that were present in the subconscious and are taken along when we pass through the portal of death affect the elemental world. Thus everything we experience after death influences the elemental world. Just like waves in a river, so do the experiences of the dead spread in the elemental world. The elemental world is constantly filled with what is aroused in it by the content of the subconscious mind we bring with us through the gate of death. What matters is to be able to bring about the conditions allowing us to see and perceive things in the elemental world. It need not surprise us that clairvoyants can recognize events in the elemental world correctly as effects of the dead. It is even possible, as you will see, to trace the effects of these experiences of the dead, which at first appear in the elemental world, all the way to the physical world — of course, only under certain conditions. When clairvoyants have gone through everything I have described and have reached the point of perceiving the elemental world, then, after a certain time, they will be able to have strange experiences.

Let us suppose a clairvoyant looks at a rose with his physical eyes and receives a sense impression. Let us further suppose that he has trained himself to develop a certain nuance of feeling when seeing the color red. This is necessary, for without it the process can go no further. Unless colors and sounds produce definite nuances of feeling, this clairvoyance directed at outer objects cannot proceed further. Suppose the clairvoyant puts the rose away. If he were not clairvoyant, what he has felt would sink into his subconscious and would be working there, making him either healthy or ill. But since he is clairvoyant, he perceives how the image of the rose works in his subconscious; that is to say, he has a visionary picture, an image of a rose. At the same time he perceives how his feelings about the rose affect his etheric or even his physical body, either in a beneficial or a destructive way. He can observe the effect of all this on his own organism. When he has this image before him, he will be able to exert an attraction on the being we may call the group soul of the rose, which underlies the existence of the rose. The clairvoyant will be looking into the elemental world and see the group soul of the rose insofar as it dwells there.

If the clairvoyant continues with this process, he sees in the place where the rose once appeared to him a kind of wonderfully shining picture that is part of the elemental world. At this point, something happens. The clairvoyant can now disregard what is before him. He can command himself not to look with his inner sight at what seems to be a living etheric being going out into the world. He then sees something that passes through his eyes and shows him how the forces work that proceed from the etheric body and build up the eyes. The clairvoyant sees forces that belong to the formative forces of his own physical body. He sees his own physical eyes as he ordinarily sees an external object. That can indeed happen.

One can follow the path from the outer object to the point where one sees in a spiritual picture in absolute darkness — no other sense impressions must be allowed — what our eyes look like. In other words, we can see our own inner organs. We have then entered the region (see diagram) that is forming and creating in the physical world: the creative physical world. We first perceive it when we become aware of our own physical organization. Thus, in a sense, we have come back full circle to ourselves. What sent such forces into our eyes that we see them as sending out rays of light, which really correspond to the essential nature of seeing? We see our eyes surrounded by a sort of yellow glow; we see them enclosed within us. This was brought about by the development of the forces that brought humanity to this point.

The forces proceeding from a dead person follow the same course. The dead take the contents of their subconscious into the world they inhabit after passing through the gate of death. Just as we can get inside, so to speak, our own physical eyes, so the forces sent out by the dead in the elemental world return to the physical world. The dead may have a special longing for a person they have left behind. This longing is at first only in the subconscious, but it soon becomes a living vision and as such affects the elemental world. What is only a vision in the physical world at the same time becomes a power in the elemental world. This power follows the path indicated by the longing for the one who is living. If conditions permit, this causes rumblings and disturbances in the physical world near the living person. The latter may hear rumbling or crashing sounds or something like that, and they are heard just like any physical sounds. Such things occurring in this connection would be noticed by many more people than they are now if people paid attention to the times most favorable to such occurrences. The best times for such observations are those of falling asleep and waking up. Generally people do not pay attention to these things. Nevertheless there is hardly anybody who has *never* perceived any signs and manifestations from the supersensible world, ranging all the way from rumbling noises to words, in the transition periods of falling asleep and waking up.

I have wanted to speak about all this today, my dear friends, to show you the nature and reality of the connection between human beings and the world. The impressions of an objective sensory world we have in our ordinary consciousness are powerless; they are as though without any real connection to that world. But as soon as what we experience descends into the subconscious, the connection to realities is established. The powerlessness of the ordinary consciousness turns into a delicate magic. When we have passed through the gate of death and are released from the physical body, our experiences are such that they are effective in the elemental world and, under favorable circumstances, even on the physical plane, where they may then be observed by the ordinary consciousness.

I have described the simplest case to you because one has to begin there. Certainly, in the course of time — and we have always taken our time gradually to work out for ourselves what we needed to know — we will move on to more complicated matters that can lead us into the more intimate connections between the world and human beings.

LECTURE FIVE
ORGANIC PROCESSES AND SOUL LIFE
July 2, 1921

TODAY I WILL have something to add to what I said yesterday. Let me remind you of something most of you have already heard from me. When we pass through death, the physical body remains behind in the earth forces, the etheric body dissolves into the cosmic forces, and we find our continuing life, our existence, in the realms between death and a new birth. I said that we can trace the formative forces working from one life into the next in the human being himself.

We know that we are in essence threefold beings with three independent members, first of all, in regard to the formative forces of the physical body, the physical organization. We have the system of the nerves and senses, extending naturally over the whole body but primarily located in the head. We have the rhythmic system, including the rhythm of breathing, circulation, and other rhythms; then we have the metabolic and limb organization, which we classify as one because our movements are intimately and organically connected with our metabolism.

You know that each person's head is shaped differently and has a unique shape. If we consider the forces that shape our head — of course, you must not think of the physical substances, but of the formative forces that give the head its physiognomy, its entire character, its phrenological expression — if we consider these forces, we find them to be those of the metabolic and limb system from the previous incarnation, which have now become form. Thus we have in the head the transformation of the earlier metabolic and limb organism. And if we consider our metabolic and limb system in this present incarnation, we find these formative forces undergoing a metamorphosis and shaping the head for our next incarnation. If we understand the origin of the human form, we can look back, as it were, through a development of the idea of metamorphosis, from the human head of today to the metabolic system of the previous incarnation. By the same token, we can look from the present metabolic system forward to the head formation of the next incarnation.[1]

This view — which plays a certain role in our spiritual psychology, just as it has in the spiritual psychology of all ages — and these truths concerning repeated earth lives are definitely not without substantiation; rather, everybody who understands the human organism can see them revealed in it. But the present trend of natural science is as far removed as possible from embarking upon the sort of investigation that would be necessary in this case. Of course, based only on the study of merely outer anatomy and physiology, one cannot help but reach the foolish conclusion that we can examine the liver in the same way as the lungs. On that basis, people put liver and lungs side by side on the dissecting table and treat them as organs of equal value, each consisting similarly of cells, and so on. This approach does not lead to knowledge of these things, and two organ systems as different as lungs and liver cannot be studied merely externally by examining their cell structure, which is what current ideas necessarily lead to.

If we really want to discover the pertinent details, we must employ methods that allow us to get an idea of these things. If we develop the methods I have described in *How to Know Higher Worlds,* then our power of cognition is greatly enhanced.[2] I have to repeat here some of what I have already explained in lectures given last autumn in the Goetheanum.[3] Our ordinary perception is strengthened, that is, the perception we use to look out through our senses at our environment and to examine our inner life, where we have an overview of our thinking, feeling, and willing. And if we expand this perception to the degree possible through these exercises, which I have often described, then our view of the outer world changes. First of all, we realize that it is total nonsense to speak of atoms the way the current worldview does. What is behind our sense perceptions, behind qualities such as yellow and red, behind notes such as C sharp, G, and so forth, is not vibration but spiritual essentiality. The outer world becomes ever more spiritual the further we penetrate in the process of perception. And so we really can no longer take seriously all those constructs derived from chemical or other ideas. All atomism is thoroughly driven from our minds when we extend our perception outward. Behind the phenomena of the senses there is a spiritual world.

However, if we look more deeply into our inner life with this enhanced cognition, there arises not confused mysticism, which can be a transition, as I pointed out and explained yesterday, but instead a psychic knowledge of the organs. We really come to know our inner organization. While our perception becomes more and more spiritualized toward the outside, our inward perception becomes, at first, more and more materialized. It is not the nebulous mystic but the true spiritual researcher who will come to know the individual organs and the complex and differentiated human organism. It is only through the detour of looking at our own inner materiality that we get into the spiritual world. Without really getting to know our lungs, liver, and so on, we cannot come to know a spiritual enthusiasm, which frees itself from the confusion of the usual mysticism and develops into a concrete perception and knowledge of our inner organs.

It is then that we come to know the structure of our soul more closely. To begin with, we learn to give up the preconceived idea that our soul is merely an adjunct to the sensory and nervous systems. It is only the world of representations that is correlated to the nervous system, but not the world of feeling. The latter is connected directly with the rhythmic organization, and the world of will is an adjunct to the metabolic and limb system. If I will something, something must happen in my metabolic and limb system; the nervous system exists to allow us to form a concept of what happens in willing. There are no nerves of will, as I have often said; dividing nerves into sensory nerves and nerves of will is absurd. The nerves are all of one kind, and the so-called nerves of will exist for no other purpose than the inner perception of the processes of willing. They too are sensory nerves.

If we study this thoroughly, we come at last to consider the human organism in its entirety. Take the lung organization, the liver organization, and so forth. As you look inward, you reach a point of surveying, as it were, the surface of the individual organs, of course, only through spiritual sight. What exactly is this surface of the organs? It is nothing less than a reflecting apparatus for our soul life. What we perceive and also what we "digest" with our thinking is reflected upon the surface of all our inner organs; this reflection represents our recollections, our memory, during life. Our memory is what is reflected upon the outer surface of our heart, our lungs, our spleen, or our other inner organs after we have perceived and digested it in our thinking. We do not even need very much training to be able to notice how certain thoughts are reflected on the whole organism in memory. All kinds of organs take part in this. If it is a question of remembering very abstract ideas, then the lung surface participates strongly. If it is a matter of thoughts colored by feeling, of thoughts that have a nuance of feeling, then the surface of the liver is involved. Thus we can describe very well and in great detail how our various organs take part in this reflection that manifests as memory, as our capacity to remember.

Clearly, then, when we look at our soul, we must not say that the nervous system alone is the organic correlate of our soul life. Instead our entire organism is the correlate organization for the life of the soul.

In this connection, much knowledge that was once present as instinct has simply been lost. It still exists in certain words, but people no longer have a sense for the wisdom preserved in words. For example, in ancient Greece, people who had a tendency to depression when remembering something were said to suffer from hypochondria, which meant a process of cartilage formation or ossification of the abdomen. As a result of this ossification, the reflection occurred in such a way as to make recollections a source of hypochondria. The entire organism is involved in these things. That is something we must keep in mind.

In discussing our capacity to remember, I spoke of the surface of the organs. In a certain sense, everything we experience strikes these surfaces, is reflected, and this leads to recollections. But at the same time something enters the organism. In ordinary life this is transmuted and undergoes a metamorphosis, so that the organ produces a secretion. The organs having this function are mostly glandular. They have an inner secretion, and the forces that enter are transmuted into these secretions. However, not everything is thus transformed into organic metabolism and the like; the organs also take up something that then remains latent within them and forms an inner force. For example, the forces developed in all thoughts connected mainly with our perception of the outer world: in thoughts through which we form images of outer objects, these forces are, in a certain way, stored in the lungs.

As you know, the inside of our lungs becomes active through the metabolism and the movement of the limbs, and these forces are transmuted in such a way that during the life between birth and death our lungs are, so to speak, a reservoir of forces that is continually influenced by the metabolic-limb system. When we die, we find that such forces have been stored up. The physical matter naturally falls away, but these forces are not lost. They accompany us through death, and throughout the entire life between death and a new birth. And when we enter a new incarnation these forces that were in the lungs form our head outwardly and impress its physiognomy on it. What phrenologists want to find out by studying the outer form of the skull can be found preformed in the lungs during the previous incarnation.

Indeed it is possible to trace the transmutation of forces from one life to the next in a concrete and precise way. And then these things will no longer be merely abstract truths, but they will be studied as concretely as we study physical things. Spiritual psychology is of true value only when we penetrate in this way to concrete facts and details. If we speak only in generalities of repeated earth lives and so forth, then these are mere empty words. They have meaning only if we can point to individual concrete facts.

Now if we cannot properly master what is stored in the lungs, it is squeezed out, as I said yesterday, much in the same way as a sponge is squeezed out. Then what should have been active only in forming the head in the next incarnation leads instead to abnormal phenomena in this life, such as obsessive ideas or even illusions. It is an interesting chapter of a higher physiology to study the strange notions of patients in the advanced stages of lung disease. This is connected with what I have just explained to you, with the abnormal pressing out of thoughts.

The thoughts that are pressed out under these conditions are obsessive or compulsive because they already contain formative forces. The thoughts we ought normally to have in our consciousness should be pictures only; they should not contain formative forces, and should not be compulsive or obsessive. Throughout the long period between death and rebirth, these thoughts are compulsive, become causative, and work in a formative way. However, during earth life they must not overwhelm us; they must not use their power until the transition from one life to another. This is the important point.

If you now study the liver in the same way I have just described for the lungs, you will discover that in the liver all those forces are concentrated that determine the inner disposition of the brain in the next incarnation. By way of a detour through the metabolic organism of the present life, the forces of the liver pass over, not into the shape of the head as did the forces of the lungs, but into the inner disposition and arrangement of the brain. Whether or not someone becomes a keen and exact thinker in the next incarnation depends upon how the person behaves in the present life, on whether via the detour through the metabolism certain forces will arise in the liver. If these forces are pressed out during the present incarnation, they lead to hallucinations or to powerful visions.

You see now concretely what I indicated yesterday more abstractly: that these things are squeezed out of the organs and then force their way into consciousness. Out of the general hallucinatory life, which should extend from one incarnation to the next, they manifest in the present incarnation and appear in the way I have described.

If we study in the same way everything connected with the kidneys and the excretory system, we will discover that in these organs are concentrated the forces that influence the emotional side of the head organization for the next incarnation. By way of a detour through the head organization, the kidneys and excretory organs essentially produce the dispositions of temperament prepared for the next incarnation. If these forces are squeezed out in the present incarnation, they lead to all kinds of nervous symptoms and conditions connected with a state of excitement, particularly inner excitement, such as hypochondriacal symptoms, depression, and so on. In short, they lead to all the conditions connected particularly with this part of our metabolism.

Everything we remember with a strong ingredient of feeling or emotion is connected with what is reflected from the kidneys. The reflections of the lungs or the liver are usually the actual ideas in our memory. If we turn to the kidney system, we see the lasting habits we have formed in this incarnation. And on the inside of the kidney system the dispositions of our temperament in the widest sense are being prepared for the next incarnation, albeit, as I said, via the head organization.

Let us study the heart along the same lines. For spiritual-psychological research, the heart is an extraordinarily interesting organ. As you know, our outer science makes things easy for itself in regard to the heart. It sees the heart as a pump that pumps the blood through the body. Now there is nothing more absurd than believing this, for the heart has nothing to do with pumping the blood. The blood is set in motion by the full agility of the astral body and the I, and the heart's movement is only the reflex in response to that movement. The blood moves autonomously, on its own, and the heart only expresses the effects of the movement caused by these forces. The heart in fact is only the organ that expresses the movement of the blood; in itself it has no active role in the movement of the blood. Contemporary scientists get furious if you speak of this. Many years ago, I think in 1904 or 1905, on a journey to Stockholm, I explained this matter to a scientist, to a medical man. He was raving mad to hear that the heart is not a pump and that the blood comes into movement through its own vitality, while the heart is simply inserted in the general course of the blood's movement and participates in it with its beating, and so on.

Something is reflected on the surface of the heart that is not simply a matter of memory or habit. Rather the life processes become spiritualized when they reach the outer wall of the heart. For what is reflected by the heart are the pangs of conscience. That is to be taken simply as an entirely physical matter. The pangs of conscience radiating into our consciousness are the part of our experiences that is reflected by the heart. Spiritual insight into the heart teaches us this.

But when we look into the heart's interior, we see forces from the entire metabolic and limb organism collected there. Since everything connected with the heart forces is spiritualized, what has to do with our outer life and our actions is also spiritualized. However strange and paradoxical it may sound to people who are clever in the modern sense, the fact remains that the forces thus prepared in the heart are our karmic tendencies, the predispositions of our karma. It is absolutely foolish to speak of the heart as a mere pumping mechanism, for the heart is the organ that brings what we consider to be our karma into the next incarnation from the metabolic-limb system — via the metabolic-limb system, so to speak.

As we get to know this organization, we learn to differentiate and to see its connection with our whole life extending beyond birth and death. We can then look into the overall structure of the human being. We cannot speak of the head in relation to metamorphoses, for the head is simply cast off; its forces were transformed in the previous incarnation and complete their activity in the present one. However, what exists in these four main systems of lungs, kidneys, liver, and heart enters the next incarnation, via the metabolic and limb system, and then works formatively, in particular shaping our head with all its predispositions. We must look inside our organs for the forces that will carry what we are now experiencing into the next incarnation.

Our metabolism is by no means a mere simmering and seething of chemicals, as in a retort, as modern physiology thinks of it. You need only take a step in walking and a certain metabolic effect is produced. The metabolism that occurs is not simply a chemical process we can examine by means of physiology and chemistry; rather, it bears within it at the same time a nuance of morality. And this moral nuance is in fact stored in the heart and carried over as karmic force into the next incarnation. To study human beings in their entirety is to find in them the forces that extend beyond the earthly life. Our head itself is a sphere, and this form is modified only because the rest of the organism is hanging down from it, so to speak.

Our head is formed out of the cosmos. When we pass through death, we must adapt ourselves to the whole cosmos with our remaining spiritual and soul organization. The whole cosmos then receives us. And up to about the middle of the period between two incarnations — I have called it "the midnight hour of existence" in one of my Mystery Dramas — up to that time we continue to expand out into our environment.[4] Gradually we become identical with our environment, and what thus goes out from us into the world around us becomes the astral and etheric structure for our next incarnation.

What determines the mother comes essentially from out of the cosmos. What is formed in the physical body and in the I enters through the father and fertilization. This I, as it is then, moves into an entirely different world after the midnight hour of existence. It moves into the world, where it can then follow the path through the paternal nature. This is an extremely important process. The period up to the midnight hour and the period after the midnight hour — both are between death and rebirth — are really very different from each other. In my Vienna lecture cycle in 1914, I described these experiences in their inner aspects.[5] If we look at them more from the outside, we must say that in the first half, up to the midnight hour, the I is more cosmic and prepares in the cosmos what then enters the next incarnation via the mother. From the midnight hour of existence up to the next birth, the I passes over into what the old mysteries called the netherworld. And via the detour through this netherworld the I finds the path through fertilization. There the two poles of the human being meet, as it were — from mother and father, from the upper world and from the netherworld.

What I am now saying was an essential part of the

Egyptian Mysteries that were based on ancient instinctive knowledge, at least as far as I know. Through the Egyptian mysteries people learned about what they then called the upper and the lower gods, the upper and the lower world of gods. And we can say that in the act of fertilization an equilibrium between the polar opposites of the upper and the lower world of gods is brought about. Between death and rebirth the I goes first through the upper and then through the lower world. In ancient times the strange nuance of meaning many people nowadays connect with the upper and the netherworld did not yet exist. In our time, people almost always see the upper world as good and the netherworld as bad. This subtle meaning was not originally connected with these worlds; they were simply the two polarities that had to participate in the creation of the world as a whole. Thus the upper world was experienced and perceived more as a world of light, and the netherworld as one of heaviness and gravity. Gravity and light were the two polarities expressed exoterically. You see, these things can be described in concrete terms.

Concerning the other organs, I have told you that the flowing out of organic forces can become hallucinatory life, and that is especially true for what is pressed out of the liver system. But if the heart presses out its contents, a system of forces is pushed out and brought to our consciousness that calls forth in us the urge to live out our karma for the next incarnation in this life. If we observe how karma works, we can say that from the human point of view, living out one's karma can only be described figuratively as a kind of hunger and its subsequent satisfaction.

That must be understood as follows: let us start from the usual view of life and look at a noteworthy event. Let us imagine a woman meets a man and falls in love with him. If this is all we see, it is like taking a small piece from the Sistine Madonna, perhaps cutting out a piece from a finger of the Baby Jesus, and looking just at that. True, we have a piece of the Sistine Madonna, but we do not really see anything. Neither do we see anything if we merely look at the fact that a woman meets a man and falls in love with him. That is not all there is to it; the matter must be traced further back into the past. Before the woman met the man, she had been in other places in the world; before that she had been somewhere else, and still earlier somewhere else again. You can find all sorts of reasons why the woman went from one place to another. There is sense and meaning to her movements though it is naturally hidden in the subconscious, but there is a connection throughout, and by going back to her childhood, we can follow her path. The woman in question — and I am not telling you tall tales — follows from the beginning the path that culminates in the event under discussion. From birth on, human beings hunger to do what they will do, and they do not give up until their hunger is satisfied. Pressing on or rushing toward a karmic event is the result of such a general spiritual hunger. The person is, as it were, driven to the event.

This is what the human being as a whole is: each has forces within propelling him or her toward later events in spite of the individual's freedom, which nevertheless exists but acts on a different plane. The forces that manifest as such a hunger, leading to their satisfaction in karma, are concentrated in the heart. And when they are pressed out prematurely and enter our consciousness during the present incarnation — that is, they still remain in the heart but we are conscious of them — then pictures of them may form that lead to excitement, resulting in maniacal rage.

Maniacal rage is nothing else than the premature living out in the present incarnation of a karmic force destined for the next life. Just think how differently we must accustom ourselves to look at world events once we have understood these connections. Of course, if you are maniacal in your present incarnation, you might boast that if God had left the creation of the world to you, you would have done a better job of it. People often ask why God created maniacal rage. Well, maniacal rage exists for a good reason, but everything working in this world can appear out of place. And this appearance out of place, which in this case is caused primarily by luciferic forces — everything that appears prematurely in the world is brought about by luciferic forces — this appearance in the earlier incarnation of karmic forces intended for a later incarnation produces maniacal rage.

As you can see, in the abnormalities of the present life we can study what is to continue in later incarnations. As you can imagine, there is a tremendous difference between what stays in our heart throughout our entire incarnation and the condition it will be in after it has gone through the long development between death and rebirth and then appears in a new life in our outer behavior.

However, if you look into your own hearts you can see pretty clearly — though of course only in latency, not in a finished picture — what you will be doing in your next life. Thus, we can say not only abstractly and generally that what will take effect in karma in the next life is prepared in this one, but we can indeed point directly to the place where the karma of subsequent incarnations is stored. These are the things that must be understood concretely if we really want to pursue genuine spiritual psychology.

You can imagine the enormous significance these things will attain when someday they are studied and made a part of general education. What does present-day medicine know of the possibility of a liver or heart disease when it does not know the most important fact of all, namely, the actual purpose of these organs? And modern medicine does not know that! It has not even found the real connection between hallucinations in a state of agitation and the kidney system, nor does it understand that the quiet hallucinations, those that simply appear and are present as I have just explained, are, so to speak, liver hallucinations. Hallucinations of things crawling on the afflicted person so that the victim wants to brush them off stem from the kidney system. These are hallucinations accompanied by a state of excitement, and they are connected with our emotions and temperament. From such symptoms a much more exact diagnosis can be made than with the methods generally used nowadays. And diagnostic methods based upon purely external evidence are very uncertain compared to what diagnoses would reveal if these connections and symptoms were studied.

Now all these things are connected with the outer world. The lungs, as an inner organ or organ system, contain our obsessive ideas and everything we take in when we perceive the outer world and then concentrate it in them. The liver has an entirely different relationship to the outer world. Because the lungs preserve the thought material, they are structured quite differently. They are more closely connected with the earthly element. The liver, where in particular the quietly appearing hallucinations are stored, is connected with the element of water. And the kidney system, paradoxical as this may sound, belongs to the element of air. One expects naturally that the lungs would be connected with this element, but as organs the lungs are connected with the earth element, though not only with that. On the other hand, the kidney system as an organ belongs to the element of air, and the heart system to the warmth element, out of which it is formed. Thus the warmth element, which is the most spiritual one, is also the one that absorbs in its tremendously delicate structures the predispositions of our karma.

Since the human being as a whole is connected with the outer world, you will realize that the lungs necessarily have a special connection with the outer world in regard to the earth element, and the liver in regard to the element of water. If you examine the earthly qualities of plants, you will find there the remedies for diseases that originate in the lungs — of course this is to be understood in the broadest sense. If you take what circulates in plants, the circulation of their juices, you will find there remedies for all illnesses connected with the liver. Thus studying the interrelationship between our organs and the outer world leads us to a foundation for a rational therapy.

Generally our present-day therapy is a hodgepodge of notes from experience. We can reach a really rational therapy only by studying in this way the interrelationship between the world of our inner organs and the outer world. Of course this means we will have to overcome the pleasurable yearning for subjective mysticism. We cannot advance to really significant therapeutic insights if we refuse to go beyond the well-known "small divine spark" Meister Eckhart speaks of, if we want only to pour out pleasure within us, to have beautiful pictures, rather than to penetrate through this element to the concrete structure of our inner organs.[6] For therapeutic insights can be acquired only on the path of true mysticism that advances to the concrete reality of our inner organism.

By way of the detour through knowledge of our inner organism we learn about our passage from incarnation to incarnation. Similarly, as we study the outer world, the world of the senses, this tapestry of sense impressions leads us into the spiritual realm. We ascend into the world of the spiritual hierarchies, which we did not find by way of the detour through inner mysticism. Instead the spiritual hierarchies are found on the path of a deeper contemplation of the outer world. The results we find on this path may at first be expressed in analogies; yet they are not mere analogies, for there exist deeper connections and relationships.

Recently I figured out for you how many times we draw breath in a twenty-four-hour period. If we assume eighteen breaths per minute, we have 60 x 18 in an hour and in twenty-four hours, in a day and a night, 25,920 inhalations and exhalations. Let us take another rhythm in human life, the rhythm of day and night. When you wake up in the morning, you draw the astral body and I into your physical and etheric bodies. This is also a kind of breathing. In the morning you inhale the astral body and I, and when you fall asleep at night, you exhale them again. Thus one complete breath here takes twenty-four hours or one day. In a year, we have 365 such breaths. Now take the average lifespan of human beings, namely, seventy-two years, and you have approximately the same result as above — a little more than 25,920. If we had started not with seventy-two, but with a somewhat lower figure, we would have had the exact same amount of 25,920.

In other words, if you look at the entire earthly life of a human being and count each day, each falling asleep and awakening, as one breath, you then have in one lifetime as many inhalations and exhalations of the astral body and I as there are inhalations and exhalations of air in a twenty-four-hour period. These rhythms harmonize completely, and they show us how wonderfully the human being is integrated into the cosmos. The life of one day from sunrise to sunset, that is, one rotation of the earth around the sun, corresponds to an inner sunrise and sunset that lasts from birth to death.

You see, we are part of the whole cosmos. And I would like to conclude this talk by pointing out an idea and asking you to think about it carefully and to meditate on it. Present-day science postulates cosmic processes in which the earth is said to have come about. Scientists say that, in the end, when entropy has run its course, the earth will be consumed in a cosmic heat death. If we base ourselves nowadays on a world-view such as the heliocentric Copernican system, or any modification of it, then we take into consideration only the forces that formed the primordial nebula and so on, and human life there really becomes a sort of fifth wheel on the wagon. Geologists and astronomers, after all, are not concerned with humanity. It does not occur to them to look for the cause of the future shape of the world in humanity itself. Human beings are present everywhere in the cosmic processes but for modern scientists more or less only as the fifth wheel on the wagon. The world processes take their course, and as far as the scientists are concerned, that has nothing to do with human beings. Just imagine if the world processes were to come to an end, were to cease and vanish into space. They would stop, and the causes of what would then continue to happen out there are always within human beings themselves, inside their skin; they will continue.

Our world here and now was prepared in primeval times

within human beings. That is how things really are. The books of ancient wisdom tell us this in their own language, and the words of Christ Jesus also point to these things: "Heaven and earth shall pass away, but my words shall not pass away." Everything that is part of the material world will vanish, but what comes from the soul and the spirit and is expressed in words will survive the destruction of the earth and live on into the future. The causes for future developments lie not outside our skin, but within us. We do not need geologists to search for these causes, but we can look for them ourselves in the inward forces of our organism that pass over into our next life and then, in other metamorphoses, into tater incarnations. Thus when you want to see the future of the world, you must look inside human beings. Everything external will perish utterly.

The nineteenth century erected a barrier against this insight, and this barrier is called "the law of the conservation of energy." This law sees the forces around us continue; however, in reality, they will all perish, disappear. Only what is still to come into being within humanity will shape the future. The law of the conservation of energy is the most false one imaginable. In reality, it does nothing else but make human beings the fifth wheel on the wagon of the world processes. It is not the statement of the conservation of energy that is correct, but the other one: "Heaven and earth shall pass away, but my words shall not pass away." These two statements are diametrically opposed. It is simply nothing more than thoughtlessness when nowadays certain members of this or that religious denomination want to be believers in the Bible and at the same time adherents of theoretical physics. This is nothing else but dishonesty, a dishonesty that claims nowadays to make a creative contribution to our culture. This dishonesty must be taken out of creative culture — which is actually anticreative — if we are to emerge from the forces of decline into those of ascent.

NOTES

LECTURE ONE

1. These lectures were: "Anthroposophie und Seelenwissenschaft" ("Anthroposophy and the Science of the Soul") of November 5, 1917; "Anthroposophie und Geschichtswissenschaft" ("Anthroposophy and History") of November 7, 1917; "Anthroposophie und Naturwissenschaft" ("Anthroposophy and Natural Science") of November 12, 1917; and "Anthroposophie und Sozialwissenschaft" ("Anthroposophy and Social Science") of November 14, 1917; all published in Rudolf Steiner, *Die Ergänzung heutiger Wissenschaften durch Anthroposophie*, vol. 73 in the *Collected Works* (Dornach, Switzerland: Rudolf Steiner Verlag, 1973).

2. Josef Breuer (1842–1925), Austrian physician. Successfully treated neurotic patient "Anna O." by hypnotic recall of early trauma (1880); collaborated with Sigmund Freud on *Studien über Hysterie* (1895).

3. C.G. Jung, *Collected* Works *of C.G. Jung, vol. 7: Two Essays on Analytical Psychology,* trans. R.F.C. Hull (Princeton, NJ: Princeton University Press, 1981), p. 20. All following quotations from Jung's work are taken from the same volume.

4. Ibid.

5. Ibid.

6. Jean Martin Charcot (1825–1893), French neurologist, known for his work on hysteria and hypnotism (which influenced his student Freud), sclerosis, and senile diseases.

   Sigmund Freud (1856–1939), Austrian neurologist and founder of psychoanalysis. Believed that a complex of repressed and forgotten impressions underlies all abnormal mental states and that revealing these impressions often effects a cure. Developed a theory that dreams are an unconscious representation of repressed desires, especially of sexual desires. Considered the mind to be composed of the id, ego, and superego. Propounded a genetic origin of motivation for basic drives (instinct theory).

7. Hermann Nothnagel (1841–1905), German physician.

8. Jung, ibid.

9. Alfred Adler (1870–1937), Austrian psychiatrist. Student and associate of Freud (1902–c.1911). Advanced theory of inferiority complex to explain psychopathic cases. Asserted primacy of aggressive instinct and developed school of individual psychology.

10. This lecture was given at Dornach on August 5, 1916. It is published in Rudolf Steiner, *Das Rätsel des Menschen: Die geistigen Hintergründe der menschlichen Geschichte* ("The Riddle of Man: The Spintual Background of Human History"), vol. 170 in the *Collected Works* (Dornach, Switzerland: Rudolf Steiner Verlag, 1978).

11. Jung, ibid.

12 Ibid., p. 80.

13 See Rudolf Steiner, "The Luciferic and Ahrimanic in Relation to Man," lecture of 1918, reprinted in *Anthroposophy,* vol. 2, no. 3 (London: Anthroposophical Publishing Company, 1927), pp. 504ff.

14. Jung, pp. 80–81.

15 Steiner here quotes from the first edition of Jung's book. In later editions this sentence was changed to "The human intellect can never answer this question, still less give any proof of God"; Jung, p. 81.

16. Ibid.

17 Ibid., p.12.

18 Friedrich Wilhelm Nietzsche (1844–1900), German philosopher and poet. Professor of classical philology, Basel (1869–79), where he was at first the friend and follower and later (from c. 1878) a strong opponent of Wagner in art and philosophy. Opponent of Schopenhauer's philosophy. Suffered mental breakdown (1889). Known for denouncing religion, for espousing doctrine of perfectibility of human beings through forcible self-assertion.

19 See lectures given in Dornach, October 14, 20, 21, 26, 27, 28, 1917, all in *Die spirituellen Hintergründe der äusseren Welt: Der Sturz der Geister der Finsternis* ("The Spiritual Background of the Outer World: The Fall of the Spirits of Darkness"), vol. 177 in the *Collected Works* (Dornach, Switzerland: Rudolf Steiner Verlag, 1985). See also lectures of November 2, 3, 4, 1917, all in *Das Faust-Problem: Die romantische und die klassische Walpurgisnacht* ("The Problem of *Faust:* The Romantic and the Classical *Walpurgis*

Night"), vol. 273 in the *Collected Works* (Dornach, Switzerland: Rudolf Steiner Verlag, 1981).

20. Arthur Schopenhauer (1778–1860), German philosopher. Chief expounder of pessimism and of the irrational impulses of life arising from the will.

21. Richard Wagner (1813–1883), German composer. Originator of the musical drama and pioneer in the development of the leitmotif. Famous for his operas, especially the cycle of musical dramas called *Der Ring des Nibelungen* ("The Ring of the Nibelung").

22. Rudolf Steiner, *Friedrich Nietzsche: A Fighter for Freedom*, vol. 5 in the *Collected Works* (Blauvelt, NY: Spiritual Science Library, 1985).

LECTURE TWO

1. Rudolf Steiner, *Von Seelenrätseln* ("Riddles of the Soul"), vol. 21 in the *Collected Works* (Dornach, Switzerland: Rudolf Steiner Verlag, 1983).

2. Max Dessoir, German philosopher and art critic. His book *Vom Jenseits der Seele (*"Beyond the Limits of the Soul") has not yet been translated [Trans.].

3. Rudolf Steiner, *An Outline of Esoteric Science*, vol. 13 in the *Collected Works*, repr. (Hudson, NY: Anthroposophic Press, 1997).

4. Rudolf Steiner, *The Philosophy of Spiritual Activity,* vol. 4 in the *Collected Works*, repr. (Hudson, NY: Anthroposophic Press, 1986).

5. Rudolf Steiner, *The Spiritual Guidance of Man,* vol. 15 in the *Collected Works* (Spring Valley, NY: Anthroposophic Press, 1983).

_____, *Reincarnation and Karma: Their Significance in Modern Culture,* vol. 35 in the *Collected Works* (North Vancouver, Canada: Steiner Book Centre, 1985).

_____, "Blood Is a Very Special Fluid," Lecture of October 25, 1906, in *Supersensible Knowledge*, vol. 55 in the *Collected Works* (Hudson, NY: Anthroposophic Press, 1987), pp. 21-45.

6. Rudolf Steiner, *How to Know Higher Worlds,* vol. 10 in the *Collected Works*, repr. (Hudson, NY: Anthroposophic Press, 1994).

7. Wilhelm Wundt, 1832–1920, German physiologist and psychologist. Founder of experimental psychology. Believed that psychology

must be based directly on experience and prescribed methodology of introspection.

LECTURE THREE

1. Steiner used the terms "imagination," "inspiration," and "intuition" to refer to three distinct supersensible faculties.
2. Helena Petrovna Blavatsky, née Hahn (1831–1891), Russian theosophist. Founded Theosophical Society together with Colonel Henry Steel Olcott in 1875. Established official journal and won many distinguished converts. Many of her so-called miracles demonstrated as fraudulent (1885) by Society for Psychical Research. Author of *Isis Unveiled* (1877), *The Secret Doctrine* (1888), and other works.
3. *Kamaloka* is a term for the "region of burning desire" or "cleansing fire", also "purgatory" [Trans.].
4. *Devachan* is a term for heaven [Trans.].

LECTURE FOUR

1. See note 1, Lecture 3.
2. See "Subconscious and Supraconscious," pp. 78–101 in this volume.

LECTURE FIVE

1. For further details see also Guenther Wachsmuth, *Reincarnation as a Phenomenon of Metamorphosis* (New York: Anthroposophic Press, 1937) [Trans.].
2. Steiner, *How to Know Higher Worlds.*
3. These lectures are compiled in Rudolf Steiner, *The Boundaries of Natural Science,* vol. 322 in the *Collected Works* (Spring Valley, NY: Anthroposophic Press, 1983).
4. See Rudolf Steiner, *Four Mystery Dramas* (North Vancouver, Canada: Steiner Book Centre, 1973).
5. See Rudolf Steiner, *Inneres Wesen des Menschen und Leben zwischen Tod und neuer Geburt* ("The Inner Nature of Man and Life between Death and Rebirth"), lectures of 1914, vol. 153 in the

Collected Works (Dornach, Switzerland: Rudolf Steiner Verlag, 1978).

6. Eckhart, called Meister Eckhart (1260-1327), German mystic. Entered Dominican order, taught in Paris, Strassburg, Cologne. Charged with heresy. Considered founding spirit of German idealism, Romanticism, Protestantism.